THE EXPERT INTERVIEWS

all about FAMILY MINISTRY

Michelle Anthony · Rob Bienow · Michayla White · Karl Bastian · Heidi Hensley · Brian Dollar · Dawn Heckert · Ste... ... Dan ... Kim Botto · Sarah Ande... ... Pray ... ...thie Phillips · Jason Til... ... ...unter · Courtney Wils... ... White ... ...Bastian ... Steve... ... De... ...erson ...lu Fr... ...Tiller ... Coon... ... Bu... Wilson ... ...elle An... ...arl Bastian ... Hensley ... ...T... Daw... ...lin ... ... a Bu... Pray... ...mily ...earn... ... ...Heck...

KEITH FERRIN

The Expert Interviews
All About Family Ministry
© 2018 Keith Ferrin
Published by Keith Ferrin Productions, LLC

ISBN: 978-0-9740023-3-0

Book Cover Design: Brian Gage, Pipe & Tabor, Vancouver, WA

Interior Book Design: Pearce Professional Writing Services, Baltimore, MD

For information or to schedule author appearances contact:

Keith Ferrin at
KeithFerrin.com
info@KeithFerrin.com

"Keith Ferrin is one of the top thought leaders of our era. His keen awareness of Scripture and how families grow together through intentional discipleship make him a sought after speaker and author. Now, in his ability to bring other leaders together to collaborate on best practices and leadership principles, this book offers the ministry leader a wealth of information in the format of sitting over a cup of coffee. I believe this book is a must read for every ministry leader navigating the landscape of today's church climate." - *Dr. Michelle Anthony*

"Keith has written a must-read for anyone in ministry leadership. His ability to collaborate and pull together the strengths of many leaders makes this book a goldmine for anyone seeking leadership growth. While great for kids pastors, this is a wonderful tool for senior leadership to better understand the current state of the families we minister to." - *Heidi M. Hensley, Children's Pastor, Shadow Mountain Community Church*

"A message that we at INCM remind leaders of is that we [the whole children's and family ministry community] are each other's greatest resource. We have so much we can learn from one another. In All About Family Ministry, Keith gathers together many voices of this community and offers to the reader their wisdom, passion, experience, and vision... and we all get to benefit from it! I highly encourage you to dig into this helpful and inspiring collection of wisdom for leading family ministry today." - *Michayla White, Executive Director, International Network of Children's Ministry*

"The power of a collaborative effort like this is that it speaks volumes as a clarion call for family ministry. Keith's dream to bring so many voices together came to life so that lifelong relational discipleship will be catalyzed far beyond any individual's ministry. We can't wait to hear how God uses you as an expert with kids and families wherever your unscripted adventure in Christ takes you." - *Dan Lovaglia, Owner, Lovaglia Consulting LLC*

"Ministry years are often marked with change due to culture, family, and resources. Keith's intentionality to equip leaders to speak into one another and share what they have learned is a fantastic tool I would recommend in every Family and Children's Ministry's leaders toolbox." - *Dawn Heckert, Director of Children's Ministries, Christ Community Church*

"I believe everyone needs and does better with a coach. I do coaching and have been coached by some amazing leaders in ministry. It has helped me improve in so many areas (especially what once were blind spots) Now Keith has taken many leaders who have been great influencers and pulled them together so that everyone can grow from the collective wisdom and experience. This is going to be a resource that will bless many leaders." - *Tom Bump*

"Keith's book is highly practical and gives us a look inside some of the top minds in family ministry. It's a must read!" - *Steven Knight, Family Life Pastor and Founder of KidminTools.com*

"You are looking at this book because you have a passion and calling to help the next generation love and follow Jesus! The heart of Jesus is for children and families! I believe yours is a front-line ministry for the Kingdom of God. This book is packed with stories and Scriptures from "fellow laborers" which will encourage and equip you. Share it with your ministry team and see what God will do." - *Dr. Rob Rienow, Visionary Family Ministries*

"Keith is one of the most genuine and 'real' people I have met in ministry. I could not be more excited about this book. The family ministry experts and messages found in this book are going to impact the family ministry community for years to come! Thanks, Keith, for sharing your relationships!" - *Brian Dollar*

Dedication

To every in-the-trenches superhero who invests week after week in the next generation. Whether you are a paid staff member, a weekly volunteer, or the person who agrees to run insane, large group games at VBS or summer camp…I salute you.

Contents

Introduction

The idea for this book came to me at a conference where you – family ministry folks – were being refreshed, challenged, equipped, and encouraged. I was one of the speakers that week, but I didn't have a breakout at that time.

So...I was walking. Praying. Thinking.

Out of nowhere (I believe by the prompting of the Holy Spirit) this thought came to my head,

"Ninety percent of the people in the trenches, doing the work of family ministry, will never attend this conference. They're volunteers who can't take time off work to come. They're at small churches with small budgets that don't include flights, hotels, meals and conference fees. And yet...these rooms are filled with experts sharing practical training that would help thousands of people who will never sit in these rooms."

Then God told me one more thing...

"Hey Keith. Do something about it."

You are holding my first attempt to do something about it.

God has graciously seen fit to put me in positions where I have gotten to know a lot of family ministry experts. We've spoken at the same conferences, worked on projects together, and shared meals. Many of them have become friends. Several I have only known by name and face (but we're becoming friends now).

When I reached out to a bunch of them and said, *Hey. I have another one of my crazy ideas.* Lots of them said, *I'm in!*

I spent the next several months gathering information, refining topics, inviting more experts, and doing one-on-one, video interviews. Those interviews have been transcribed into the chapters in this book.

A quick note: There is no "right order" to read this book. I put the experts in alphabetical order by name. Read this introduction. Take a look at More Than Just A Book. (It'll be easy to find. It's on the next page.) Then scan the Table of Contents and pick the topic that interests you most right now.

This book covers a lot. That's because these women and men know a lot. And they have generously agreed to share it all with you.

I can attest that every one of these experts agreed to do this because they want to see you flourish. They know your successes and trials because they've also walked (and still walk) the family ministry journey.

They did this for you. I did this for you. You are the reason this book exists. In fact, you are the reason the church will thrive in the coming decades. Why? Here are a few reasons…

You are passionate about families.

You equip.

You cheer.

You train.

You teach.

You listen.

You pray.

You celebrate kids.

You support parents.

Families are healthier because of you.

Churches are stronger because of you.

And Heaven will be more crowded because of you.

God gave me the vision for this book while you were on my mind. May the words on these pages encourage, inspire, challenge, and equip you to keep doing what you're already doing – loving and serving your Heavenly Father by loving and serving His kids.

Alongside…for the whole family.

Keith Ferrin

More Than Just A Book

You might not realize this, but what you're holding is not just a book. That last sentence isn't some emotional statement about the awesomeness of the content (although I can brag a bit about it, since 99% of the words in this book are from the experts, not from me).

This is more than just a book because owning this book gives you free access to the All About Family Ministry Online Portal.

I have asked each of the experts to share downloads, book recommendations, websites and other resources related to their topics. Our ultimate desire is to equip you to go deeper in each of these topics.

Inside the All About Family Ministry Online Portal you can:

- Watch the video interviews

- Download free resources

- Get book recommendations from the experts

- Find links to other resources

- Discover how and where to interact directly with the experts

All you need to do to access the All About Family Ministry Online Portal is:

Go here: KeithFerrin.com/AllAboutFamilyMinistryBook

Enter this password: FamilyMinistry (case sensitive)

Enjoy!

Let me know if you find any broken links or have any resources we should add on a specific topic. After all, we're in this together.

One final note: Obviously, it would be easy to share this link and password. I'd rather have you share the book. Giving someone the book will help me fund future resources. If you simply don't have the financial resources to send someone a copy, please email me their name and address. I would love to send them a free copy.

Thanks.

Keith

THE INTERVIEWS

How do I help kids fully participate in the life of the church?

I have with me today Sarah Anderson from Cincinnati, Ohio. Thank you so much for participating in this interview.

Yes. It's my pleasure.

Just to set some context for those people reading this who don't know you, what is your children's ministry journey, and what context are you in right now?

Yeah, so my journey started really quickly. I became a children's pastor about two and a half years ago, and soon after that I became our regional children's champion for the Vineyard movement. So there are about 40 churches that I help with their children's ministry as a reference, a resource for them.

I am also a teaching pastor on staff at our church, and this past January I got to speak at the Children's Pastors' Conference for the first time. My church is Vineyard Church Northwest in Cincinnati, Ohio, and we have about 700 people on a Sunday morning, usually around 120 kiddos each weekend.

What kind of church environment did you grow up in?

I grew up in a Presbyterian church. Really great, thriving church. Really awesome youth group, awesome Sunday school. I went to church camp every summer, and it was a really great growing-up experience.

Good, good. Diving in now... You use this phrase where you talk about helping kids and equipping kids to "be ministers and to worship fully." Before we dive into how we equip our kids to do that, I'd like to hear a little bit more. What do you mean for kids to "worship fully?"

Right. I am passionate about this. I obviously had a great experience growing up, but I wasn't necessarily equipped or released to minister and worship was... It was a nice part of Sunday mornings, but it wasn't a life-changing experience for me. Within the past several years while I've been here at this church, I've really learned what it means for me to worship fully and how worship can be transforming and I've been equipped to minister to other people and that was really transformative for me as a person.

And I really think the kids are the church of today. They're not the church of tomorrow. We're not just building into them for who they're going to be as adults, but they have the power to change the world today. So we really need to give them these skills of engaging in worship so that it is transforming their lives and giving them tools and skills and even practice so they can be equipped to go out into their little world, their playground, their school, their home, and really minister to those around them.

Yeah, as I've known you for a little while and heard you talk about this, this idea of kids who worship fully becoming those that minister fully, and that those really go hand in glove with each other, for sure.

Even before we dive in, I know we didn't talk about this question, but with your role helping out 40 different churches, and as you've now had the opportunity to speak at CPC and connect with people from a broad range of churches and denominations, do you find that this is something that isn't on people's radar, or it is on people's radar but they just don't know how to do it, or they're resistant to it? I'm just curious at what you feel like the tone of churches is when it comes to this topic of really equipping kids to worship fully and minister fully.

Right. I think this is a new frontier. I don't think a lot of people are doing this. I don't think a lot of people are talking about it. My experience, even within the Vineyard, and the Vineyard has a heart for this, but even within our movement, not a whole lot of people are plugged into it yet.

There has been, I wouldn't say resistance, but there's been a little bit of a light bulb moment for some people of, "Oh, the kids can do this?" Then I share testimonies of how it's played out in our kids' ministry, how it's played out in different kiddos' lives, and then they start to press into it step-by-step. Then they see even more, "Oh, the kids really can do this!"

Yeah, cool, cool. I'm glad you're seeing more of the "light bulbs" than getting resistance.

Yeah.

Because it's so, so necessary. All right. Diving in, then, to the equipping piece, what would be the practical tips or steps you think others can take to even begin equipping children within their own ministry, since it's really the children's pastors and volunteers and children's ministry workers who this is aimed at?

First of all, I would say take some time to decide what your values are, or what your denomination's values are, as far as evangelism or healing or praying for others stands. Because different denominations think different things. In the Vineyard, we have a real heart for healing prayer and for praying for other people and laying hands on people, so in my context, that's our value. But in your context the value might be different.

It might be a value for evangelism, for sharing the gospel with people. Decide on what your values are and then how you can put a structure around that. Even just being kind, reaching out through being kind to other people and giving kids some skills for how to do that.

Then, I would recommend you develop a prayer model or an evangelism model or a kindness model. Develop a quick model that has a couple steps in it that are really practical and easy to remember for the kiddos. For instance, our Vineyard prayer model is actually the one that the adults use. We use the exact same thing with the kiddos. It's really easy. The kids know it. Step one is to say, "How can I pray for you?"

Step two... I always tell them step one-and-a-half is to say, "Is it okay if I touch you?" Because you don't want to just put your hands on people.

Right.

Step two is to invite the Holy Spirit. "Holy Spirit, come." Step three is to pray. Step four is to check and say, "Hey, how are you feeling? Are you feeling any better?" Then step five is to pray again or set another time that you can pray with that friend. The kids know these steps.

Every year we take about a week for each step, or five weeks total, to go through and review each step in the process and why it's important and how to do it with kindness and how to do it confidently. The kids know these steps, even some of our three-year-olds. When they pray for somebody, they'll say, "Can I pray for you? Holy Spirit, come. Pain, go away." Rapid fire. [Laughs] But they know it, and they get it.

The faith of a child.

Yes! So, develop a model that's easy to remember, that the kiddos can get in their heads and they can remember to do it. It really will take some time. You'll have to devote some time on Sunday mornings to do that as your lesson so that it really gets integrated, because I know we all have kids that miss weeks. We don't have perfect attendance from our kids, so if you take six weeks to review it and to go over each step, they'll get it. By the end of the six weeks, you've hit enough of the kids that it will start to become integrated into your culture of your kids' ministry.

Then, make it a part of your Sunday routine. For us, we do a time of extended worship, and I can talk a little bit more about that with how we worship, but at the end of worship time we enter into ministry time. We do a couple loud and rowdy songs that the kids really get into, and we jump and we shout and we sing and it's really great. Then we have a quieter song where we just enter into really thinking about Jesus and how amazing he is, and then we flow right from that into ministry time.

Each week, the kids are practicing those five steps of praying for each other, of praying for the leaders, the leaders pray for the kids, and it's just this really cool time of everyone in the room being in a place of power and being in a place of being able to minister to each other, and it's really neat. Building it into your Sunday morning routine on a consistent basis will help the kids be comfortable enough to take it outside of the church. It'll become like second nature.

Good, good.

I was thinking of the example of telling somebody, "Hey, you really should cook, and you should really cook in this method," and then never giving them any time to practice it. The chance of that person leaving your house and going home and actually using that method to cook is slim to none, but if we provide a place for the kiddos to actually practice what we're teaching them, it almost becomes a bit like roleplaying, especially for our younger kids.

We pray for a lot of boo-boos that are mostly healed already, but it doesn't matter, because the kids love it. They feel loved, they feel encouraged, and it gives them a chance to practice it. No matter what you want to encourage the kids to do, whether it's "How do you stop a bully on the playground?" "How do you stand up for a friend?" "How do you encourage a friend who looks sad?" There are lots of different things that we can build into our programs, and we can put a little bit of structure around it to take some of the fear out of it and then give the kids a chance to practice that in class. That's what we do as adults. We need time. We need to learn how to do something and then we need time to practice it before we're willing to step out on our own.

Great. I'm curious. Early on in the conversation, you talked about those "light bulb" moments. For a children's pastor who's at a church where this is something they want to explore, this is something they want to approach their lead pastor with or their board of elders or however their structure is, how would you even start the conversation at a church that isn't doing it yet? Would you just start it within the children's ministry? Would you try to start it with the whole church? What input would you have for how to start?

Yeah, so I think there's a two-fold method here. I really believe that you'll know what a church is about if you look at the children's ministry. If a church says that it has a value on healing prayer, but the kids never do healing prayer, it's probably not really a value. I look at children's ministry as a barometer for what the church really values. Churches that have a really high value on biblical knowledge, those kids can recite the 10 Commandments. They're reciting memorized verses all the time. You can use kids' ministry as a barometer.

But I think the flip side of that is that kids affect their parents, and that affects the adult side of the church. I think for our church, healing prayer really is a focus for the whole church, and so the fact that our kids are doing it is showing that that value is really taking root in the whole congregation.

But we also have families where the kids go home and the kids demonstrate how to do this to the parents, and then the parents are encouraged to step out and take that step of faith, and the children are becoming the leaders. I think if you're at a church where this is something totally brand new, don't be afraid to start it just with your kiddos, because kids can change things, and it infiltrates into the home and then that's going to infiltrate into big church. And eventually, change could come and that's why I think it's also so important to stay within the values of your denomination.

Not every denomination has the same values as the Vineyard, and so it doesn't have to look the same in every church, but if you're staying within the values of your denomination, within the values of what your specific church is really going after and just putting some practical structure and steps around it, it's going to be much more well-received.

Good. That's what I was really wondering, whether you felt like it could be something that a children's pastor could just start with their small group of kids, even if it's a volunteer children's pastor at a church with eight kids. Do they need to get buy-in from the whole church before they start or whatever? But I love that you're saying that you can start where you are and see how it can grow from there.

Definitely.

Wonderful. Thank you so much, Sarah. I appreciate this. I think helping kids become fully engaged in worship and become ministers, not just the church of the next generation. I think that my heart leapt as you said one of my favorite phrases, really, early on, of "The kids are the church of today, not the church of tomorrow." I think that is the framework for all of this conversation, for sure. Thank you so much, Sarah!

Thank you.

Sarah Anderson

Sarah Anderson is a national kids leader for the Vineyard movement and a children's pastor in Cincinnati, Ohio. She is a dynamic speaker and teacher. Sarah is passionate about equipping kids to do kingdom work and helping them to encounter God in real ways. Sarah and her husband, Grant, have been married for thirteen years and have three amazing sons.

How do I equip the leaders—paid and volunteer—in my ministry?

I'm here today with my good friend Dr. Michelle Anthony. How are you today Michelle?

I'm doing fantastic actually. It's a beautiful day here in Colorado.

Before diving into something that you are both passionate about and gifted at – which is equipping leaders – give us the lay of the land of your children's ministry journey so far, and what context you serve in now.

Sure. I was really privileged to grow up in a church that had an excellent children's ministry. That was pretty rare in that era and I'm thankful for the focus my church placed on children. My heart was captured for Jesus at a young age. When it was time to go off to college, I chose a Christian university where I studied Christian Ministries. Went on to get further education to really help me understand the educational practice of that, and also the development of children and teenagers.

My very first church job was an internship in junior high ministries. But then, I had children shortly after that. I had always wanted to do youth ministry exclusively, but then I began to realize that those young developmental years were so important after having my own children. My husband took a position as a family pastor at a church, and so they looked at me and said, "Hey, we get two for the price of one! Will you lead the children's ministry?"

After about five or six years there, I was hired to run children and youth ministry at another church. There, God really captured my heart for family ministry, and involving all the generations. Especially equipping parents to be the spiritual leaders of their home. It's been about 30 years now, that I've been doing some form of ministry with children, youth, or families. Currently I'm serving as the family pastor at our church here in Colorado Springs.

Great. Let's dive into equipping leaders. I have had the privilege of watching first-hand as you pour into the lives of your team, and your volunteers, and the adults who surround you at conferences. The ones who are then going to go serve kids. When it comes to equipping leaders I know that you're passionate about developing them. When did you first develop that passion for knowing that equipping leaders is important if you're going to serve families?

For me, it was when I was working in a ministry context that was larger than my bandwidth. The demand was bigger than something I could physically do myself. I realized I needed to replicate myself. In order to replicate myself, it meant that I was going to have to spend an enormous amount of my time and energy pouring into other leaders so that our ministry could exponentially grow. It was about that time I realized, "I'm not going to be spending as much time with the kids as I have in the past."

That is a big transition for a lot of people who take positions of leadership. You start ministry with kids or students, because you love kids or students! But, as you grow as a leader, your job really becomes investing in other people that you are replicating your own leadership in, so that those kids and students are ministered to.

I think it was that transition from that smaller church where I could kind of be all things to all people, to a larger church where I needed more of me in order to minister to those families and those children.

Okay. While you and I could talk for hours about how to equip, and why to equip, I know you've boiled it down to a few absolute essentials when it comes to equipping leaders. Unpack those for us a little.

I regularly use three words that embody my philosophy. That model is Inspire, Equip, Support. Let me just talk a little bit about each one. The first one is Inspire. For me, this has to come first. It has to come first because this is the place where we cast vision for our leaders. We tell a story of an envisioned future. Our leaders come in because they're willing to serve, or they want to help out. They want to use their gifts. But then, we must have a compelling place that we're taking them. Moses did this in the Old Testament when he was telling the Israelites about a land flowing with milk and honey, right? He's casting a vision. He's saying, "It's not like the desert, it's this other place that God has for us. It's the Promised Land. We'll be free to worship God alone!"

So, we cast a compelling vision and we inspire people to think of something that could be more than where they are now. I think also, we inspire our leaders when we call out certain qualities in them. I love to address leaders and say, "God has really fashioned you to have a voice that teaches truth." Or, "God has put his heart in you for the outcast, or the vulnerable. Make sure you lean into that, and you never lose that." Or, "God has given you an authority when you speak."

Whatever those things are, we call out those qualities, and then we link them to that envisioned future. Then they feel a part of that journey. And they're inspired to go on this journey because those qualities will be needed in the "promised land" of where we're going.

Another way that I love to inspire leaders is to bless them. Using blessings to speak truth, or wisdom, or Scripture over their lives. Sometimes I do it very formally at the end of our meetings, or at the end of an event. But, often times it's just organic, when we're walking or working together. Blessings good words of truth spoken to that person. I believe that's something we need to grow in as a Christian community.

Then I would say the final thing about inspiration is that it cultivates tradition. You inspire people when you have certain traditions, and things that they can count on. One of our traditions is something that's called, "Remember and Celebrate." After a season, or after an event, we'll take time to remember how God has shown up, and showed His faithfulness. Then we'll celebrate the goodness, both in each other, or all the wins of things that took place. But, my team knows that's a tradition. They look forward to it! "When are we doing the remember and celebrate?" "Where will it be?" they ask.

Those are the kinds of things that build an ethos, and a comradery, so that the team isn't just following you. They're also following one another in this kind of group or tribe. They have a belonging and ownership. So many leaders are looking for that. Nobody wants to just go on this mission to an envisioned future by themselves. They want to do it with a team of people, to be known, and loved, and belong to something bigger than they are.

Absolutely. I've seen you put each of those in action. It's fun hearing you talk about it so succinctly, because I've seen all that lived out. That idea of inspiring both with the vision casting, and with the personal piece of it. I think that second part, and third part – the traditions – gets lost so often. That a leader understands, "Yes, I need to cast vision. Yes, I need to lead people in a direction." But, I think so often that part of speaking truth into the individual to make them even believe they can be a part of that vision coming to reality is something that often times gets lost in the shuffle. It is so vital.

It is vital, and it has to be intentional. You've said them quite well. We cast a vision, we tell them the part they're playing in it, and then we show them why they need each other.

Mm-hmm (affirmative).

You're right. If parts two and three don't happen, then you might get to your goal by yourself and realize no one followed you there.

Right, exactly. I remember somebody saying, "If you're leading and have no followers, you're just on a walk." [Laughs] All right, so what is the second essential after inspire?

The second essential is to Equip. I can inspire you all I want. I can pump you up, and I can, "Rah, rah." But, until I equip you to do what I've asked you to do, that inspiration might fall flat. The equipping part says, "I'm going to give you practical tools to help you achieve the goal that I'm asking you to do." I could tell you right now, "We're going to go climb a 14,000 foot mountain." I can inspire you all I want, but until I train you to do that, you probably won't be successful at it.

My time of equipping is varied, because it depends upon the goal. Sometimes there's a short term goal, and sometimes there's a long term goal. My equipping can be determining what our values are. Our values are how we will make decisions. Equipping you with that means that you can make a decision in my absence, because you know what I value. Essentially, this is what Jesus has done for us. We don't have Him telling us what to do in every situation, but we know what He values, and we know what is truth. And so, we are capable of making decisions in His absence, with the help of His Holy Spirit, which we also have.

Yes.

Equipping might be a time where I am diving into some hermeneutics with my team, because they need to have confidence of how to study Scripture. A lot of our leaders haven't gone to seminary, or had those kind of tools. And so, that's also a big part of it. I also teach them very practical things. For example, when a parent, or a volunteer, or somebody else comes and has a question. We don't answer in the negative, we answer in the positive. We don't say things like, "You can't go in those doors." We say, "The outside doors are available for entering and exiting." We don't say, "You can't have your younger children with your older child in the same classroom." We say, "Your children can be together this week, and next week they will be in their age appropriate classrooms."

But, we take time to practice, and equip them with language that is appropriate for their job, or their mission. I call it "not getting sucked into the vortex of an emotional conversation" with a parent when they're disgruntled about something. We practice how to affirm that family member. How to say, "Those values are very important to you, and I can understand why. Let me share with you a little bit about our vision and what we do offer here." It can take on different forms. Sometimes it's a practical tool, or a class online that they have to take because they need to know how to reconcile a budget. And sometimes it's interpersonal skills. Sometimes it's spiritual, or theological. But, that's essentially my job. To equip those who I'm leading to be effective and efficient in their job.

I could see it being really helpful for a family ministry pastor or leader to get together for a long lunch with some of the more seasoned volunteers, to just walk through some of these areas. For example, if somebody was brand new to the check in process, to the lesson time, to the game time, to the parent handoff at the end, to the weekly event, to the big event, to the VBS. If they sat down and listed all the different places where anybody's going to be interacting with a kid or a parent and said, "What ways could we equip them in that?"

Mm-hmm (affirmative).

So often, for people who have been in ministry for so long, or have been volunteering in their church for a long time, so many things become second nature. We forget what we didn't know the first year!

Right. Exactly. And, even if somebody is shadowing me, I will explain everything along the way. I'll tell them why I'm doing what I am doing.

That's great. Ok, what's the third essential?

The last one is Support. We've cast this vision, we inspire them to their place in that mission and with this team. Then we give them the necessary tools to succeed. Then, support recognizes that along the way, they're going to stumble. They're going to fall. They'll grow weary in well doing. They will become discouraged. The enemy will attack them. A number of things will get them either off track of their mission, or forgetting the inspiration they had at the beginning. And so, support begins by me praying for each of my leaders by name. Praying for them, and with them.

Also, my team knows that they can take a mental health day. They don't have to pretend they're sick or come up with an excuse. They can let me know, "I just really need a day to decompress, or to be with the Lord." We call them "Mental or Spiritual Health Days." Soul care is important, and I need to support them in that. I can't guilt them. I can't respond in a way that makes them feel that they are "less than."

Or, it could even be a family health day. Because we are in children and family ministry, it would be wrong for me to have them sacrifice their marriage, or their children for the sake of what we're doing at church. Sometimes a leader will call and say, "My kids are having a meltdown today. I need to take them to the mountains, or to the park." I need to support that, and trust that they'll get their work done.

Or, "I've been really neglecting my spouse. We need to go away for the weekend. Can I have this weekend off?" Absolutely! I need to be able to support that. I think also, support takes the form of encouragement, and admonition. This is biblical right?

Indeed!

Then, we encourage and admonish. Encouragement, obviously. I think we can be good at those things, and speaking good words over them. But, I also have to have the right, as part of my support of you, to admonish if I see trends, or bad habits, or sinful behaviors, or reactions. And so, sometimes I'll tell my leaders, "Let's be aware of your face. Your resting face. Let's have more cheerful disposition." Or, "You've been coming in late week, after week, after week. Let's address the root issue of that." Or, "The way that you responded perhaps wasn't the best. It felt defensive. I want you to succeed in this mission we're on. These are some of the things that will help you in that."

Good.

Admonishment is part of that. Another huge part of support is me empowering them to do the job the way that God has gifted them, and wired them to do it. If I micromanage this mission, they will lose the joy of the mission because God has uniquely gifted them, and equipped them. So, I need to empower them. Often times I will stretch my team to do something before they think they can do it. Then I tell them, "I trust you to do this. If you need me, please let me know. But I trust you to be able to do this on your own." When it's done, even if it's done differently than the way I would do it, I need to celebrate their win, and empower them to possibly take on something they wouldn't have taken on at that moment.

Yeah, yeah. I think that word, "trust," may be a good place for us to wrap up. So much of all three of these are a building of trust. As you inspire people and they see you doing it, and they see your passion, they'll start to trust you more. If they come to experience that you're equipping them, and you're providing them the resources, the tools, the training that they need, they're going to trust that the next time you call them to something, or assign something to them, that you're going to equip them to that.

Encouragement obviously builds trust. But, admonishment. If the inspiring and equipping is not happening, excuse me. Then, somebody's not going to even be ready to hear the admonishment. But if they see how much truth, and how much blessing you're speaking into them, and they know that you're training them, and teaching them well, and leading them well. Then, when those admonishments come, they're never fun. But, they're better received.

I love the whole idea of creating a culture of Inspire, Equip, and Support. I love that! Thank you so much for taking the time to hang out with me on this, and unpack it. I'd like to have another three hours!

I know! It's my pleasure Keith.

Dr. Michelle Anthony

Dr. Michelle Anthony is the Executive Pastor of Families at New Life Church and Dean of Youthmin Academy. She is the author of *Spiritual Parenting, The Big God Story, Becoming a Spiritually Healthy Family, A Theology of Family Ministry* and her newest book, *7 Family Ministry Essentials*. Michelle has over 30 years of church ministry and leadership experience in children's and family ministries and graduate degrees in Christian Education, Bible and Theology from Talbot School of Theology and her Doctorate of Education from Southern Seminary. In her free time, Michelle enjoys being with her family, reading a good book, and the beach while drinking a strong cup of coffee.

KARL BASTIAN

How do I help kids become "participants" instead of "spectators"?

I'm here today with my good friend, Karl Bastian, from Colorado. Thank you so much for being here.

Absolutely. Excited.

You and I talked about so many different topics we could explore. This idea of taking kids and shifting from them being "spectators" to them being "participants" is such a vital topic. Before we dive in give us a little bit of context. What has been your children's ministry journey so far and what context do you serve in now?

You know I got into Kids Ministry via a pretty unusual path. I literally started as a kid. I saw this awesome evangelist when I was a kid. He had a huge impact on me that week and at the end of the special week, I told my mom, "That's what I'm gonna do that when I grow up!" and my mom said, "You start next Wednesday!" Shocked, I replied, "I said when I grown up," but she replied, "If God's called you to Kids Ministry what's growing up got to do with anything?" So, literally the next Wednesday she had me up in front of the kids in my very first teaching opportunity and I've been doing it ever since!

Eventually, I guess they just start paying me to do it, but for years - all through junior high, high school, college, I was teaching Sunday school

ot or teaching kid's church. That lead to my first children's pastorate. I'd
never heard of a children's pastor! When I became one, I thought
I'd made up the term. It was a really new thing. I've served church
plants, I've been in some large churches. My favorite's the churches
that are medium to small ones where I've got a hundred kids to teach
on Sunday and along the way I started Kidology.org which is just a
website for sharing how to minister to kids within the context of their
world. I love to study their culture, their humor, their toys, because
having started in ministry as a kid, I of course knew what kids liked
because I was one but as I got older I didn't want to lose that knack for
know what kids like. Even the apostle Paul said that when he became
a man he got rid of childish things. Well us children's pastors, while
hopefully we do mature, we want to retain that child-likeness. It's the
key to connecting with kids.

That's been my journey. I've been in Kids Ministry for decades, literally
since I was a kid. I can take my age - which I won't tell you, just subtract
10, and that's how many years I've been in children's ministry!

*Good. OK, diving right into turning spectators into participants.
Sometimes – as people stay longer in children's ministry – some
people let their volunteers or their staff do the teaching. You've always
maintained that you want to be up front and be teaching and be
involved in that. Why is that so important to you?*

You know, first I want to say no criticism to anyone who doesn't teach.
We all have different gifts and different abilities and some are great
administrators and some are great teaching, but for me, personally,
I have to be in front of the kids teaching. That doesn't mean I don't
build a team and I don't share that privilege with others but I kind of
make the joke, "Can you imagine a church being run by a pastor who
didn't preach?" As the kid's pastor, the pastor for the kids, part of their
spiritual journey is them knowing their pastor, it is them getting to
know my heart and they get to know me personally and I'm sharing
with them what God is teaching me. I went full-time with Kidology
for many years and many people said, "Boy, Karl once you get a taste
of being full-time with a non-profit, you'll never go back to that week
in and week out ministry." I definitely can relate to that, the freedom I
had, but I missed teaching and getting to know individual kids. I had
to get back to teaching kids. Honestly a big part of it is simply that it's
so much fun.

What are some of these lessons you've learned and these principles for turning spectators into participants?

Yeah, that's one of my favorite phrases. When people say, "You know we follow you on Kidology or YouTube and you're a great teacher and what's your secret?" I do have some guiding principles. One of those is you don't demand attention, you earn it.

Another one of those is this turning spectators into participants. So that's what I would love to talk about because we go to big church and we sit. We participate in the worship maybe, but for most of the sermon, the bulk of the service, we are watching the screen or watching what's happening on the platform and kid's church is church for kids but some days I just greave when I seen them just take the adult model and do the same with kids. Kids can't sit and pay attention very long.

We all remember screen savers right? We may have them on our computers, but the reality is we don't need them anymore. But the idea was if you didn't touch your mouse or keyboard something went up on the screen to save it. Well, kids have these mental built-in screen savers. If you're not nudging them through curiosity or imagination or humor, an internal screen saver goes up and it might be what I'm going to do this afternoon. They might start thinking about a favorite TV show or video game. You've got to constantly be nudging them. The best way to do that, to draw their attention back continually is through participation. I try to make sure I'm not talking more than three or four, five minutes tops before something happens that the kids are involved and are interactive.

We had a patriotic lesson a couple of weeks ago from July fourth. We were talking about how we vote for Jesus by the choices we make every day. He's the King. He doesn't need votes. So we did this vote with your feet thing where I had some things up on the screen. If you like McDonald's, go to this wall. If you like Burger King, go to the other wall. We went through different sodas. We went through vacation places, video games so the kids were all moving back and forth but then I talked about what it means to vote with your feet. We choose everyday by the choices we make whether we're choosing Jesus or choosing something else. If I just started talking about that, it would have fallen flat.

Just last Sunday, we're in a series on choices and the importance of the choices we make. I wanted to talk about that inner battle and get into Romans 7 and Galatians 5:17 but if I started talking about it it would go right over the kid's head. I had to ask myself one of my guiding questions is, "What can I do?" What game can I play or activity can I provide that will get the kids engaged in something that is basically like a activity object class? We did a thumb wrestling game. I joked about how I wanted to be on the thumb wrestling Olympics team and then I found out there wasn't one. The kids had to pair up and do the, "One, two, three, four. I declare a thumb war." We narrowed it down to one kid and he was the champion but then I had him fight himself, which was kid of funny. It was so fun. I said, "You got to make it look good," but I said, "If your right thumb wins, you'll get some candy, a handful of candy. If your left thumb wins however, I'm gonna drop a book on it". He had a choice between reward and pain. He did a really good fake battle but of course he chose to let the right thumb win.

But, then when I talked about the inner battle and nobody was surprised that his right thumb won. He had the power to choose and he chose the best thing so I said, "Every time we do something that's against God's Word or His will, it brings pain and when we do the right thing it brings reward." But, they experienced it. That was the key. We talked about sin being like a fire and stop, drop and roll and had the kids literally come up and demonstrate stop, dropping and rolling. I picked my most hyperactive kids to come up and act that out but then we talked stop sin drop not literally but pray, "God help me not to do the right thing," and then roll, move away from the temptation.

Whatever the lesson is I'm asking myself what can I do to get kids out of their chairs, up on front and doing something either in the chairs or upfront or as a whole group? They came in curious because there were stickers on all the chairs and I had a spinning wheel. I said, "You made a choice when you came in today of which chair you were going to sit in and there's consequences." I spun a wheel and as it landed on the color of their sticker the got a little treat. Just constantly and any time I feel like I'm losing them I would go to that activity.

You try to keep it moving. Keep them involved and it keeps them on the edge of the seat. We've probably all have that frustration where we ask the kid, "What'd you learn last week?" They answer, "Uh, I don't know." Parents ask, "What'd you learn in church today?" They get the same answer. So I coach my parents to ask the kids instead, "What did you DO in church today?" Kids can remember what they DID and then as they share the game or share the activity, the parents can often figure out what the lesson was about. It's just so beautiful and powerful to get them involved.

Yeah. Looking at a couple of different things you've talked about... There is the engagement piece. How do we keep them engaged and instead of keeping us talking? Then that piece of "coaching the parents." The conversation the kid has with the parents later about what they did. They're certainly going to remember more of what they did versus what they learned. And as they talk about what they did, it's going to be reinforcing one more time and cementing what they learned in their hearts and minds. And honestly, as a parent, that's a more enjoyable conversation.

Exactly. You know a pastor succeeds if we can repeat back his three sermon points, right? For kids, knowledge is assimilated. It's not filed. It just becomes a part of who they are. I've had parents literally call me during the week to say, "My kid did something strange this week, a good strange. What did you teach about last week?" Then I'm able to explain what the challenge was or what the activity was because you think you failed if they can't repeat what they learn but you haven't. It's just become a part of who they are. I like to say kids learn by what they discover, not what they're told.

You want to teach on something like justification. If you say, "Okay, kids. Today we're going to learn about justification. Justification is just as if you never sinned and our positional ... " Oh, man. You might even lose the adults. But, if you let the kids discover that by playing hangman and I call it un-hangman. I do it in reverse because, as I joke, we don't hang people at church! Or you put the letters in a balloon and they have to pop the balloons and unscramble the word or whether they're under the chairs and they all look under the chairs. Whoever's got a letter come upfront and try to unscramble it. I have them discover the word and if it's a big word like that they're going to have a hard time unscrambling because they've never heard of the word so you're coaching them through. Then they've really got that word down.

Any way you can get the kids involved in the learning process or even create an experience. I know a teaching on missions. One time I did a thing where I said I'm going to throw out some chocolate kisses. You have to stay in your seat, though. I love you guys all. I want to give you all a kiss. I was throwing candy out but I was throwing handfuls to the front row and just one or two to the back. The kids in the back were getting angry because it wasn't fair. The kids in the front were turning up their shirts and hoarding the candy.

Then I ran out of candy and I calmed them down and then I said, "Well how did you guys in the back feel?" They described unfair, I didn't get one, I only got one. Kids in the front were very happy and I talked about the plenty we have in America, more than we need and how around the world you know I don't need to give you the whole lesson. You can figure it out but the bottom part was then I prayed over the kids and commissioned them as candy missionaries to go into all the room and to share the candy. Every kid ended up with candy.

Even the fact that it still wasn't fair was a good learning activity that they didn't have all the same number of pieces because life isn't fair. But, they all got to experience sharing from their excess. Well that kind of experience helps them learn what it was like to be given to, what it was like to give. Then when you talk about why we give them missions or why we go on mission trips and why we do all these things now they get it because they've participated in a part where they felt the emotion of whatever.

Well I could do a lot longer podcast than you have time for but they can always just go on Kidology.org because of what I'm passionate about, posting things that will draw kids into the learning experience because that's how they learn. Kids can stand up and be objects. They can hold things. You can do instant skits where you're telling the story but the kids are acting it out but you want to ask yourself what experience can I create? How can I get the kids out of their chairs and get them involved in the learning process? It doesn't always have to be super spiritual. You can do something as simple as fruit basket where the kids all have to get up, run around the room and get back in their chairs. That will completely hit the screensaver and get them back engaged.

Definitely. We just have a little bit of time left and I would imagine that some people who are reading this, or watching this interview, hear about the examples you give and are tempted to just write it off as "Well, Karl is just one of those guys that's an idea factory." While I've known you long enough to know that in some ways that's true, you and I both know that one thing about children's ministry people is that they love sharing ideas. When it comes to finding these activity-related ideas – we'll certainly put links to different resources and I know you've got a ton on Kidology – but this is kind of a two part question. How much time do you spend each week either researching or coming up with the engagement piece? And what are some of the places where you find that inspiration that would really be accessible to anybody at any sized church on any budget?

I love writing. I love teaching. For years, I would just write my own stuff and much of that's available in Kidology but I also have seasons like I'm now where I run a larger ministry and I've got lot of stuff to do so I use a curriculum. Whatever curriculum you use, there's no perfect curriculum. I mean I adapt the lessons every week because as I read through what another creative person put together, I look at the big idea, I look at their games and a lot of time I'll use what they have or I go how can I blow this up? How can I make it just a little bit better or bigger or a little crazier or a little out of the box?

But, I probably only spend two or three hours a week planning my lesson. I try to do that early in the week so that if there's some props I need to buy or something I can do while I'm already at Walmart any way but it's really just studying it through and asking those simple questions: What will get them out of their seat? What will get them participating? What will they think is crazy fun? What will engage them?

Another example from last week, as they came into church they were offered up, there was a huge bucket of candy and the leader greeting them said, "You can have a piece of candy or you can have this coupon for two at the end of kid's church." They had to decide between the immediate gratification or more if they waited and I don't need to explain how that attacked in the lesson but it was no wrong answer. Half the kids took a piece of candy and were content. The other half said, "I'll wait until the end and get two." The parents loved it. As the parents were coming in, I explained to the parents the choice that they faced as well.

Really, it's just asking the right questions, going through whatever curriculum you use. Obviously, there's games online but a lot of times it's not hyper creative. People often say, "Where do you get this idea?" Well, a lot of times, I'm taking a basic classic fundamental idea and just putting a fresh new twist on it.

We grew up in Sunday school with the erase-a-word where the teacher would write the Bible verses on the board and we'd say it over and over as she erased a word. Most of us don't even have black boards anymore but we can do a PowerPoint where a funny graphic covers a word. I've put words on balloons and gone down with a needle and popped the balloons, put them on pipes, put them on boards, put them on whatever! And it's the same concept, just a fresh new spin. It's new to the kids!

A lot of times the games and things you're doing aren't actually hyper creative, you just put a spin based on your ministry theme, based on your curriculum's theme and you're just twisting it a little bit. Networking like you said is important too. There's a zillion Facebook groups out there now. Go in there, "Hey, I'm teaching on this, anyone have a fun game for that?

Right. I see that on your Facebook group all the time! Somebody just says, "Hey, I'm teaching this lesson. Has anybody found a creative game to teach this?" And bam, they've got 20 different ideas!

In my own Kidology Facebook Group, you'll see that I'm not the end all creative person. I post all the time in there this is what I'm teaching. "Here's what my puppet's going to do and I need ideas." I love that my ministry benefits from those that share with me as much as I try to share what I'm doing. I'm learning as much as I'm trying to help others.

Absolutely. And that's probably a great place to end. This idea of learning from each other and sharing with each other and ministering to each other. Because we're in this together. So often I find – especially for people in children's ministry at smaller churches, you can feel alone. It may just be them planning the whole lesson. Or they might have one volunteer who might show up on Sunday! But coming together in that community you realize that the children's ministry community is a very generous community. I love that idea of learning from each other and sharing ideas.

Don't feel like you have to blow out all the stops every week. Sometimes I do crazy insane things but I can't do that every week. You become your own worst competition. Ministry's a roller coaster. You want to have those crazy weeks where you go outside and just have kid's church outside or you bring in a live animal or something. Every week should be fun and interactive and creative but it's okay to have a rhythm to where there's three or four regular weeks but every now and then you got to be willing to just do that crazy over-the-top thing - because those are the lessons that kids will talk about years from now. They'll be high schoolers in your church coming up to you and going, "Do you remember when you ... " and they'll describe your whole lesson because it was one of those the top of the roller coaster rides on that Sunday and they remember those things.

Right. Thank you so much. You and I could talk about crazy, creative ideas ad nauseum! Thanks for taking the time Karl. I really appreciate it.

Hey no problem. Thanks so much.

Karl Bastian

Karl Bastian has over twenty five years of experience as a full time children's pastor in large, small, and mobile churches. He is the founder of Kidology.org, one of the first and still leading Internet destinations for those who minister to children. He is the host of *KidminTalk.com* a popular children's ministry podcast and widely known as the creator of *ToyBoxTales.com*. He is a prolific writer of training resources, books, magazine articles and is the author of *DiscipleTown*, the children's church curriculum from *DiscipleLand. com*. Karl has a Bible Theology degree from Moody Bible Institute and a Masters in Children's Ministry from Trinity Evangelical Divinity School. Named by Children's Ministry Magazine as one of the top twenty influencers in children's ministry in the past twenty years, Karl is a trainer and encourager at conferences around the world, but his favorite place to be is in front of kids creatively teaching them the Bible and training them to serve God. In his workshops or one on one coaching Karl brings the joy of children's ministry to life and with it, creative and practical ideas and principles that will recharge your ministry. Karl's life mission is to Reach and Teach as many children as possible with the Good News of God's Love and in the process to Enlist, Equip and Encourage others to do the same. He is currently the children's pastor at The Rock in Littleton, Colorado.

KIM BOTTO

How do I work with the "difficult kid"?

I am here today with Kim Botto and I am so thankful that you are here. Thanks for joining me.

Thanks for inviting me, Keith.

For those who may not know you, what is your background? Give us a little bit of your KidMin journey if you will.

Well I've always loved kids. Kids have always been a part of my life, but I majored in business and got an MBA in finance and found that wasn't what I was called to! I've been on staff at three different churches of varying sizes and the role that I'm currently in is at Crossroads in Cincinnati where I lead the kids and student teams. That's birth through 12th grade. We're a multi-site church so we have 14 sites and then I also lead our adoption and foster care initiatives.

The other churches that you were at, what were the different sizes since there will be people watching this and reading this of all different sizes?

Oh, gosh there was probably one that was about five hundred, another that was a couple thousand. Crossroads where I'm at now, we have about five or six thousand kids birth through fifth on a weekend so 30-35,000 on the weekend.

Okay so I've heard you talk about "That Kid." Tell me more about who "that kid" is before we dive in how to go about serving them best.

Any of us who've served with kids have had times where there's a kid in our ministry that maybe when they don't show up, we're not disappointed. [smile] We might even celebrate the fact that they're not there. A kid who we put all this time and effort into this amazing experience and they're disruptive and they take us off task. That's the kid I'm talking about.

Gotcha.

But God really banged me on the head and showed me that's actually my favorite kind of kid.

Oh yeah? [Laughing]

Yeah. Yes it is.

How long were you in the ministry before you discovered that that was your favorite kind of kid?

Well, to tell you the truth they've been my favorite kid for a long time but what I didn't realize is I thought they were everybody's favorite kid. One day, somebody said to me, "Did you ever notice when you're running into a room other people are running out?" I replied, "No, I never noticed." Yeah, so I do enjoy kids who have a hard time fitting in.

That's certainly a huge issue. Now, for the children's ministry leaders and volunteers that are going to be watching this or reading this, where do you start? How do you train your teams and volunteers and staff to work with "that kid?"

Well first of all, just a little bit of our journey as a church. Every year we go away and we pray individually and come back as a team to share "What's God calling us to?" And sometimes it's all over the place and sometimes everybody's hearing the same thing.

Back in August in 2012, people were coming back and they're saying, "I see kids with disabilities." "I see kids that aren't welcome in other places being welcomed here." And so…that's awesome.

Then God started fulfilling that vision and we had kids coming in that we didn't know what to do with them. Their behavior was so challenging and so disruptive. So what we did is we went to school and learned how to better respond to them.

What we found, we did a lot of study on trauma through Trauma Competent Care, Empower to Connect and also Jayne and David Schooler. And what we learned in that is the old ways of discipline simply don't work with kids who've experienced trauma. The first thing we had to do with our volunteers is give them some information, data to show them that kids who've experienced trauma, their brains are wired differently than a child who has been in a more stable environment and because of that the old ways of discipline simply don't work with them. We have to learn new ways of responding.

The first part of what we have to do with our volunteers, we have to build up some empathy for kids who are challenging and then also show them that we have to learn new ways because, Keith, and I'm sure you've worked with people who have been in ministry for years they're thinking, "I've been in ministry for 20 years. I know how to handle kids. I know how to do a time out." I go back and then I challenge, "Okay 20 years ago, what kind of car were you driving? How were you preparing your food? What TV shows were you watching?" Everything has changed in the past 20 years including the environments that our kids are being raised in. We as a church need to change the way we respond to them.

Indeed. Indeed, yeah. Whenever you stop and you actually start looking. Even around your room or your house. Or the fact that we're conducting an interview from thousands of miles apart and, at least on my end, the audio and the video is crystal clear.

Right.

When I was a youth pastor that wasn't happening.

Well look at this thing. [Referring to her smartphone.] This thing is glued to us now. Twenty years ago it wasn't. Yeah, times have changed.

Indeed. So, diving into the meat of what you and I talked about – and why I wanted you in this book – is for not only the "recognition" that things have changed and that those kids, "that kid," needs to be served and the volunteers need to be trained on it, but I'd love to hear your ideas for WHAT you train them on. What are some skills you can build, some ideas that you have that any KidMin leader or volunteer can put into practice?

Okay. What we try to do when we do train is we give very simple, practical ideas that the volunteer or staff can use the next time they interact with a kid. While these strategies were developed for kids who have experienced trauma, they work with all kids. I've got some kids that I adopted who came from trauma and others that I gave birth to, they work with all kids.

One of the big things around here for us is, and we learned it from Karyn Purvis, is "Connect Before You Correct." When a kid is not behaving as we would want them to, often our response is to go to discipline, the correction piece. And so what we train in is connect with that kid first.

For example, if a kid comes into your room and they're just crazy out of control as soon as they get there, because you know we've got a lot kids with ADD and things where they're super high energy, rather than immediately telling them, "Stop. What are you doing?" We connect with them and say, "Hey, Keith. I'm so glad you're so excited to be here today. Let's walk over to the table." Or if we have these kids that punch a hole in the wall, rather than immediately saying, "What the heck are you doing?" We go up to them and say, "Gosh, Keith you seem really angry. Can you tell me what's going on?" It starts breaking down those walls that that kid has built up. What we want to do is to get to know the kid and have a relationship with them and "Connect Before You Correct" really helps form a relationship.

Good. So...

You want other ideas?

Yeah. I know that you and I, as we've exchanged emails, you talked about some ideas. A few that I'd love to unpack a little bit are the idea of "offering options," the "power of yes" and "the do-over" and what you mean by those three.

Okay what we like to say is, "Offer options or a choice." See options or a choice. An example of that would be, and this is an example that happened with me: We had a fifth grade boy who was sitting in a large group and was so disruptive kids around him couldn't pay attention. It was disruptive to the teacher in the room so I went to him and rather than just tell him, "Hey, be quiet and sit still," which he simply may not have been able to do, I gave him an option. I said, "Hey, you can come to the back of the room and walk back and forth during large group or I'll get you a chair and you can sit back here. Which would you want to do? Pick one." He chose to walk back and forth in the back of large group.

The really interesting thing was, when the teacher started asking questions, he could answer every single question. He couldn't just sit and listen. He needed to be moving while listening and then when his mom came to pick him up – I didn't know her – I was at a site I wasn't normally at, and I said, "Hey, are you Tommy's mom?" She immediately looked down at the floor because I'm sure she's had people, when they're asking, and they have no positive things to say. I told her what a great job he had done, listening and responding. She started to cry because she had terminal cancer and she ended up dying a few months later.

I think remembering that every kid has a story and they're often hard stories, but by offering that kid a choice he was able to fully engage. And it works with preschoolers. If you're ever doing a large group of preschoolers, they all want to be on the stage. You tell them, "Do you want to put your feet on the stage or do you want to put your hands on the stage while you sit there?" It's amazing how many of them pick one of those options and then that's what they do.

It works with spouses too. In case you needed pointers on that. [Laughs]

[Laughing] Perfect. I will take that note.

Another one that we train in is "the power of yes." You know Keith, if you ask somebody a question and they respond with a "no," that ends the conversation. There's no more conversation when that happens. But, if we can look at ways to say "yes" to kids, this doesn't mean that we're giving them everything that they're asking for, but we're responding in a positive way.

An example could be when you used to do kids ministry, do you give snacks in the preschool room? A lot of preschool rooms give snacks and that's a much-anticipated treat for the kids. You have a kid that says, "Can I have my snack now?" Rather than say, "No," you say, "Yes, you can have your snack. I'm going to put your goldfish right up here on the counter and I'm going to put your name on it. As soon as we come back into small group, you can have your snack."

Or if the kid says, "I want my mom right now." Rather than saying, "Your mom's not here," you say, "You can have your mom. See that clock over there? When this hand on the clock gets to here. Your mom will be back." The power of yes is real. Kids hear "no" a lot and so being able to answer in a positive manner is helpful.

That's great.

Going back to the choices thing. Another thing you'll hear, we as adults often want to be in control and sometimes as adults we feel like we're giving up that control if we give a kid an option. But we're not, because the only options we're offering are options that we're okay with.

Right, absolutely.

Another strategy that works really well is the "do-over." And that's simply if a kid does something and it's not the manner which is the socially acceptable manner to do it. Let's say you're walking by a group of kids and one hits a kid on the head. We don't want that. We don't want physical force in our children's ministry rooms.

We can go to that kid and rather than scold him for what he's doing and tell him what he did wrong, we tell him how to do it right. Let's use a girl example. We tell Suzy, "Hey, Suzy can we walk back again and then use a gentle touch with Tom when we go by?" Suzy can walk by and maybe pat him gently on the back. Or often in kids ministry we have kids who run everywhere and if they run from large group to small group rather than say, "Don't run," we'd say, "Hey, when we go from large group to small group we walk. So let's try it again and you're going to walk." What it's doing, it's training them in the right way and so when they leave our rooms, they leave having the last thing that they did they did it correctly.

I always played tennis in high school and I was horrible. But the more times that I practiced my serve the better I got at it. The more opportunities we give kids to do something correctly, the better they're going to be at it and that's what we're after. We're not after short term compliance. I don't want to get them just to comply in the moment. I want to train them long term and so do-overs are really helpful in the long term training.

That's good. I really like that. We're not looking for short term compliance. We're looking for long term success.

Right.

That's worthy of putting on the wall!

That's true with our own kids. I think also when there's an infraction when the kid doesn't behave in a manner in which we hoped, don't look at it as an opportunity to discipline instead look at it as an opportunity to build a relationship with that kid. That doesn't mean we let them run wild and we let them do whatever they want to. But really the end goal is relationship. Because in order for them to understand what a relationship with Jesus looks like, they need to understand what a relationship with people in their lives look like. For some of these kids that come through our doors, they don't have any positive relationships.

Right, the end goal is relationship. I think that's a terrific note to end this interview on. Keeping that end goal, the beginning with the end in mind. All of these strategies that you've given really lead to that so I'm so grateful that you would share and participate in this project.

Thank you.

I look forward to seeing what God does as more and more people learn these strategies and start really loving on that kid.

That's right. Thank you, Keith.

Yeah, thank you.

Best to you and your project also.

Thank you. Thank you. This is exciting. New endeavors.

Yup. Thank you.

Kim Botto

Kim leads the kids and student teams at Crossroads Church, as well as their initiatives around adoption, foster care and vulnerable kids. Crossroads has sites in Ohio and Kentucky. Kim's passion is creating fun and safe environments for all kids regardless of their background, energy level or unique needs. She also serves vulnerable kids and their families through community training and advocacy.

How do I last for the long haul?

I'm here today with Tom Bump. Thank you so much for joining me, Tom.

My pleasure. Good to be with you, Keith.

Before we dive into this topic of "leaders that last," give us a little bit of background on your own ministry journey and what context you serve in now.

Well, I've been in the ministry for a little over 30 years now, but really all my life. I'm a preacher's kid, so I moved around and spent a lot of time in a lot of small churches. I mean, we're talking a hundred people or less, sometimes 150…maybe. [Laughs] So, I grew up in a lot of small communities, small towns, and got involved right away with ministry. I also served with Child Evangelism Fellowship as a local director. Started out as a 19-year-old director in Indiana and Michigan.

God used those experiences to call me into local church ministry, and so I've been a youth pastor, an associate pastor, children's pastor. I've kind of been a little bit of everything in the church, but in churches that have ranged anywhere from, like I say, a hundred to 700, to where now I'm in a multi-site church of five churches, serving 5,000 people. The campus that I'm at is a young campus, only four years old, and is averaging about 400 people right now.

It's been an amazing journey of a lot of ups and downs. A lot of heartbreak, but a lot of joy and excitement to see God work. It's just been a cool journey that He's taken us through.

Yeah. You've been in ministry for three-plus decades, so you've experienced longevity in ministry. Why are you passionate about helping others do the same?

I think the reason why I'm passionate is because I really believe we have so much left to do. For me, there are still so many people that need Jesus! I feel like we need good, strong leaders who are in it for the long haul, because the world needs to see that serving God is so worthwhile. That it's our calling, and it's what we want to do, and it's the only thing we want to do.

I see a lot of young leaders who get discouraged. And it wasn't what they thought it was going to be, and they abandon ship quickly. They leave. We're seeing pastors and leaders quit in record numbers, and that's just heartbreaking to me. I mean, my father has been in ministry for 50-some years, 60 years, and still wants to keep going, and running, and gunning. He's always been my inspiration to say, "He can do it. I can do it." But I want others to do it as well. I want them to see that God desires to use them for the long haul.

Before we dive into how people can last for the long haul, let's quickly looking at the flip side of that. What do you think are the two or three main reasons why leaders quit too soon?

I think, unclear expectations. I think, pride. I think, competing vision. I think, unrealistic vision. I think those are the key categories. You see a lot of things where people just thought, "Oh, hey, ministry's going to be like this." Then they get in it, and the reality is totally different on the other side, behind the curtain so to speak, that they didn't expect it to be. Maybe they got in for the wrong reasons, because they thought it was going to be this one glamorous lifestyle. I mean, nobody gets in it for the money, so it can't be that! [Laughs]

I think there are these unclear, unmet expectations. I think, like I said, sometimes it's our pride. We think, "Well, we should be in the bigger and the better." We don't get that attention, and so we're not content to serve where God asks us to serve. So, a lot of people just get discouraged, and they let those things get in their way and creep in, and it pushes them out the door, rather than staying around for the long haul.

Okay. So, staying around for the long haul. That's our theme. That's going to be our hallmark. You've seen in your own ministry how you've been able to last 30-plus years. But, as you've been in ministry that long, you've also seen other leaders last.

Yes.

What have you learned about those leaders and how somebody that's reading this – who is maybe a year in or three years in – that could really help them last?

Well, here's the thing. I think it really comes down to four keys. We'll talk about this in more depth in a minute, but there are a couple of principles that I think that lead to those keys. One is that those leaders take care of themselves. And two, they take care of others well. When they do those things, it builds into their ministry the power, and the influence, and the ability to lead when they do those things right.

Now the four keys. The first key that I've learned from other leaders, and I've learned in myself, is calling. One of the things that I've seen very clearly is that leaders who last for that long haul know why they're in ministry. That is a bedrock! For me, I knew why God called me in and how he called me in to ministry. And that "why" for me keeps me going.

There's a little girl in Detroit, Michigan who came to Jesus. God used that little girl to speak to my heart very loud and clear. I knew that's why I was being called into ministry, to reach children. So, for me, calling is huge. I think that's really, really important, that they're clear on, "I'm called to reach children," or "I'm called to reach students," or "I'm called to reach people with the gospel." I think that's very, very important.

I think another key area that I think is important is the giftings we have. I think a good, strong leader knows their gifting. They know what they're good at…and what they're not good at. We all have talents and abilities. I think a leader who's secure in that calling and secure in that gifting doesn't sit there and try to compare themselves to other leaders. It's easy to play the comparison game. It's easy to look around and say, "Well, I'm not as gifted as that person" or "I'm not as gifted as that person."

One of the things I learned and came to understand very clearly for my own self is that God wired me a certain way, with a certain personality, a certain temperament, a certain ability to do certain things, and I needed to be content with that. I needed to be okay that that is how God has wired me. That's what he's gifted me to do, and I'm going to do what I do best!

When I learn that ability and I stay in that lane, I can then take the things where I'm weaker and hand them off to other people and delegate. I think that's a mark of a good leader. If they know their giftings, they know how to delegate, too, because they know that, "If this is my weak spot, I need to give these other things away." It's not that I don't ever want to develop them. I do. I keep working on areas where I'm not as gifted, because I want to improve myself. I want to be a well-rounded leader. But I think it's important for us that, when we consider our gifting, we truly know, "This is how God has wired me, and I'm okay with that."

I used to compare myself to other leaders, especially when I was in a smaller church. I'm like, "Well, boy, if I was able to do this..." Sometimes we forget what gifting is and we look at the resources, and we start comparing sizes and all this kind of stuff. That's, really where, again, it can mess us up. Our pride gets in the way, and it can cause discouragement.

I'm blanking out on who said it, but I just recently heard somebody quote somebody else in saying that, "Comparison is the thief of joy." [Note: It's from President Theodore Roosevelt.]

That's good. That's good, "... the thief of joy." It really does. I mean, it can mess us up when we start looking at, "Boy, why didn't I get wired this way? Why am I not as good administratively as other people?" I have some people that. Man, it just seems like they're naturals at organization and the admin stuff. Well, I'm a creative type, and I love people, and I love being around people. I would much rather be sitting in a room talking to people and sharing what I've learned than sitting down and planning a spreadsheet for Bible school. Spreadsheets give me hives, man! They're terrifying to me, because that's not my gifting. My gifting is not that way.

Some people are terrified of doing big events, where other people, that's where they thrive. They love being within 48 hours of Vacation Bible School, because that's when they get the most done, and that's the way they're gifted. Some people love lists; some don't. I think leaders who are going to be in it for the long haul know that they're okay the way they're wired, and they're secure in that, and they don't have to compare themselves to other leaders to say, "Well, if only I was like this, I'd be a better leader."

No, you're a great leader the way God wired you! Be that leader that God wired you to be and then lean in to other people. Use the resources, leverage the resources, that others have, and honestly you're going to be developing other leaders that way, too. So, it's a good thing to have.

Now, so you said there were four of these key areas. We looked at calling and gifting. What's the next one?

Priorities. I think a good leader for the long haul has to have very clear priorities. I think we all get this. I think this one is one of those that people will be going, "Yeah, Tom, I get that." The thing is, we talk a good game about priority setting, but the thing I'm talking about is keeping them and having accountability in keeping them! You've got to not only know your end goal as a leader, where you're going with your ministry, but also where you're going as a leader, where you need to grow, your blind spots, and you need to know your focus.

So, having clear priorities in your relationship with God, in your relationship with others: to your senior leadership, to your team. You need to have clear priority of who's in charge, and who's doing what, and "Who do I answer to?" Having priorities of where you're going, and how you're going to get there, and seeing those steps of what really is important so that you don't get distracted. I think a big mistake I see a lot of leaders making nowadays is that they jump from thing to thing to thing. When senior leaders look at those of us who are sitting in the supposed "2nd or 3rd Chair" on the team, if they see us hopping all over the place and not having clear priorities set, it creates this distrust. It can really undermine your credibility with not only your senior leadership, but with other leaders as well that are trying to serve with you.

So, I think leaders that are really good leaders from the get-go set clear priorities and say, "This is what's important to us, and we're not going to get distracted." No matter what gets presented at the next conference as the latest and greatest. Maybe that doesn't fit for you, and you need to know. I mean, I know people that just jump! As soon as somebody promotes something, they're on it and thinking, "Oh, I've got to have this. I've got to use this." It may not even fit them! If you don't have clear priorities, you're going to get swept around, and you'll exhaust yourself. So, I think clear priorities of knowing exactly where you're going and how you're going to get there is huge.

Before we move on to the last one...I think this priority piece is big. I agree with you that people will kind of head nod and go, "Yeah, that's a good idea." Now that you've been doing this for over 30 years, how often do you re-evaluate your priorities? How often do you visit them? Do you have them posted somewhere? Do you journal about them? Do you share them with your team? Give us another 30 seconds if you can add a little bit of "how-to" of priorities.

Yeah, I think you hit it really well, because it does need to be real clear. If you're going to have priorities, they do need to be posted. I think you need to evaluate them on a consistent basis. For everybody it's going to be a little different. For me, as I'm planning my calendar, they're in front of me. I've got them posted in my home office. I've got them in my church office. My wife knows them. My senior leader knows them. So, I have accountability with several people. I have another accountability group I share with them. They're to ask me once a month if I'm doing it.

So, I think for every leader it's going to look a little different, but I would post them. I would keep them in front of you. I'd set little reminders that can pop up on your calendar to do that. I honestly say one of the best things you can do is put your priorities up there and then look at your calendar and say, "Is it matching? Am I doing what my priorities are, or have I put other things in higher ranking, where they shouldn't be?"

I think you've got to be very clear about getting some good accountability on a regular basis, whether you need to set it up weekly, once a month, quarterly. I do try to take a quarterly break, where I'll take two days and look through my to-do list, my priorities, and those kind of things, what's coming up, to make sure I'm staying in line, because it's so easy to get going all catawampus and spinning out of control.

All right. So, this final one as we bring the ship into the dock: What's the fourth key?

That fourth key to me is having clear boundaries. It kind of ties them all together to me, because your calling, and your gifting, and your priorities all come together in helping you shape boundaries. Then you know: When do you need some Sabbath rest? When do you need a sabbatical? Like I mentioned, for me, my boundary is I set a hard date quarterly where I'm taking two days off to get alone with me, and my Bible, and my journal. I get out into the wilderness, and it's just me and Jesus. I'm just going to be a son of God, and that's it.

I know that's my boundary. I've got to set that up, because if I don't schedule it, I won't do it. So, I set boundaries as far as when I'm available online, when I'm not available; when I'm available to my team, when I'm not available; what I will do and what I won't do.

One of my boundaries is I don't do child care. My campus pastor came to me recently and was like, "Hey, would you be willing to oversee the child care for this one event?" and I went, "No, I don't do child care. Here's a list of some names of some people I know who can do it. Why don't you call one of them?" He came back the next day and was like, "Hey, so-and-so is going to take over child care for this event."

That's my boundary. I know where I need to be, where I need to focus on what I'm good at and what I'm called to do, what my priorities are, what my giftings are. When you set those clear boundaries, you almost have to have a to-don't list, not just a to-do list. There are some things that you just have to say, "I won't do that. I'm not going to do that." Again, I don't want that to come off prideful or arrogant, because it's really not. I will serve my leader however he needs, but that was the best way I could serve him, because if I started doing that, I'm going to be away from doing something else that I need to be doing.

Have a real clear boundary of, "This is what I do. This is what I know I can do. This is what I can say yes to. This is what I can't say yes to." Know those things.

If I get a call to speak at a camp, well, if it's in this certain time frame around an event, I know I have to say no, because that's my boundary. I know that I will exhaust myself, and I won't be sharp and ready to go.

One of those boundaries I emphasize a ton to young leaders is Sabbath rest. Taking care of yourself physically, mentally, emotionally, spiritually. Having clear boundaries set in those areas are huge.

Absolutely. So, calling, and gifting, and priorities, and boundaries, clarity in those four key areas. This has been great, Tom. Thank you so much for taking the time today.

Oh, my pleasure. Thanks for having me.

Tom Bump

Tom is a veteran ministry leader of 30 years who's served in various sized churches. He's served with *Child Evangelism Fellowship* and has a M.A.R. in Pastoral Counseling. He's the founder of Elevation Coaching Group, whose purpose is to help equip, encourage, and challenge leaders to take their leadership and ministry to higher levels. He's a husband and father of four young adults and loves to read, go camping and he's also sports nut!

REV. MELISSA COOPER

How do I create and grow a multi-generational culture at my church?

Well, Melissa, thank you so much for joining me today.

My pleasure. Glad to be here.

As soon as I was told about you, I was excited about your passion for intergenerational ministry. But before we dive into this important topic, give us a little bit of your background on your journey in family ministry, and what context you serve in now.

Most of my ministry career has been spent in camp and retreat ministry, so I have spent most of my time hanging out with kids of all ages, as well as adults. I spent my last six years or so at a retreat center, doing mostly adults and family camps, intergenerational camps there. My background is actually in youth ministry, so I spent a lot of time there, and ended up having a really interesting experience at the first camp that I served at. One of the first weeks of camp that I was there for was actually a family camp, and going into it I thought it was the worst idea I'd ever heard of. It was so much more fun just to have the kids. I was just looking forward to being done with that week so that we could get back to the good stuff.

I found myself absolutely enthralled by seeing what multiple generations, spending time at camp together, could look like. Families of three and four generations at camp together, worshiping together, playing together, hanging out together. That was sort of the very beginning of my journey.

Since then, I have just dug deeper into "why." Why was that important? Why did that matter? Why did that seem to be such an important part of their experience? From there, I've spent a lot of time doing camp and retreat ministry with intergenerational camps, but also that has led me into doing a lot of resourcing of churches, of consulting, of coaching.

That's now what I do full-time, which is as an associate with an organization called Vibrant Faith. We're an ecumenical organization. We do a lot of resourcing of churches, through things like coaching, and consulting, and research, and projects in that way.

Okay, great. You used the phrase "intergenerational culture." As we were talking beforehand, different people will use the phrase "intergenerational ministry" or "intergenerational culture," and mean lots of different things. To kind of level-set us, what do you mean when you say "intergenerational culture?"

I think that's one of the most important pieces of this whole conversation. Sometimes, some churches I work with, this is all they need, a definition. To really understand what they're talking about, and then they can envision what that looks like for them. One of the things I have tried to do is to almost eliminate the term "intergenerational ministry" from my vocabulary. It's not because it's not a valid term, but I think a lot of us, because of the way we do church, when we hear terms like "intergenerational ministry," we think about adding something else to the calendar. If there's something I know about most of our churches, it's that we do not need something else on the calendar. We're not lacking things to do!

The concept of "intergenerational culture" encourages a shift from a program-based mindset of church to a culture-based mindset of church. The way that we approach church affects everything else. If we approach it as a collection of programs, that's what it's going to look like. The shift to thinking about how we bring generations together and do intergenerational work really works better when we think of it as a culture. My friend John Roberto likes to use the word "ecosystem," to think about not just the what that we do but the why, the how, the big picture. It's not hard to conceive of how to do an intergenerational program.

I can give you a pretty decent formula for putting together a family camp or putting together an intergenerational night. But that one program is not going to develop lifelong faith in our young people or in our adults. When we think about what really does develop faith, what really creates a lifelong yearning, a desire, to be part of a faith community, to be in relationship with God, it all comes down to something much, much bigger than a single program. I've heard somebody describe culture as "the water that we're swimming in." You don't know that you're swimming, what culture you're swimming in, until you're suddenly flopping around on the beach, as they say. When we think about what is the water that our churches are swimming in, is it focused on a series of programs or is it focused on developing a real culture that builds faith?

That idea of lifelong faith, anybody reading this book or watching this interview is nodding their head at the idea of building lifelong faith rather than just getting a kid to check off the, "I believe in Jesus. I believe in the Cross. I believe in the empty tomb. Now, we're done." We want this lifelong faith, and so that really leads to that question: Why is intergenerational culture so important for our children and for building lifelong faith?

What's funny is I get the opportunity to come into churches and talk about this as though it's a new idea. In reality, my job is so easy because it's not a new idea. It's something that is the way church worked for a very long time. A lot of us who grew up in the church, particularly our older generations, they know what this looks like. This isn't a new concept because this is how many of this were in fact formed in faith. One of my favorite activities to get people to do is to talk about their faith story. What key moments do you remember? What key realizations do you remember coming to?

Almost every time, when people tell those stories, they talk about people of other generations. They very seldom say, "Oh, I was in a group of teenagers and we all came to realize... " That isn't usually the story. That isn't usually the key place. There is usually somebody else, somebody usually of another generation, who impacts their faith formation. Who impacts why they are a Christian now, why they attend a certain church, why they have a passion for what they do.

This idea of separating kids out, and doing these separate things that are just for kids, is a relatively new concept. When we look at the last 50 to 100 years of faith formation, we see us, little by little, separating out kids from the rest of the church, to do things just for them. Now, it comes from a really, really good intention of wanting to meet kids where they are. I don't ever want to say that's wrong! That is not at all the intention. But what ends up happening is, as we pull them out to the point that they never interact with that intergenerational faith community, that is how so many of us are formed ... If you also follow the patterns of lifelong faith, of young adults continuing in their faith, of young people continuing in to attend church, showing signs of mature faith, those have begun to dwindle as well.

It's not that there aren't other reasons for this. I'm not saying children's ministry is killing the church by any means. But the way that we are doing children's ministry, a lot of times, is contributing to our young people leaving the church when they graduate high school. I think what we see is we see young people who have been a part of a phenomenal children's ministry. They've been a part of a fabulous youth group. But they've never actually been part of a church.

They need more than just people of their own age to be able to really grow in faith...lifelong. We forget this is how we were formed too. We forget that. In the name of doing the best thing for kids, often, we actually remove some of the most important things for them. Really, the reasons we've done this is as much about us as it is about them. A lot of times, kids not being in worship, we say it's because we want them to worship on their level, but in reality we want to worship in peace. We don't want that turmoil. We have to own a little bit of our own complicity in all of that.

We can look to our own stories. We can look to our own faith stories. We can look to the history of the church. But I am a big fan of looking at data. There is so much good research out there that helps us really frame why intergenerational ministry is so important for our young people, specifically. The Fuller Youth Institute has done some of the best work around this. Their Sticky Faith research a few years back was really good. Most recently, they've done work with churches growing young. They were the ones that told us that 40-50% of our youth group graduates were leaving the church, and they weren't showing back up.

It's not that a young adult exodus is a new concept, but they're not coming back when they have kids, like they used to. We've got to ask the question, "What have we done? How have we contributed to that concept?" Also, they discovered in that same piece that family and parents are the most influential part of a child's life in their faith formation. If a child is not spending time in those faith-forming activities, like worship, like reading Scripture, with their family or with other adults, then they're missing the most influential piece of their faith formation.

Okay.

One more. [laughs} My favorite bit of research is actually from the Search Institute. They have done work on child and youth development. It's actually in a secular setting. They're not looking at faith. What they have discovered is that every young person, for their most successful development, needs a minimum of five adults, five unrelated adults, in their life. Where better to get that than the church? Even if we're not looking at faith formation, we are talking about the betterment of our young people. When you add faith into it, you can't go wrong.

Definitely. For the children's or family ministry pastor that's reading this, or the volunteer, or the leader, who says, "Okay, we're not doing that right now," what are these first steps that they can take?

The biggest one is, to be an advocate for some of this, you do need to be able to read about this, to study it, because a lot of people know it in their heart. A lot of children's ministers I talk to know in their heart that something's missing. That something's missing when the kids that they love the most aren't engaging the rest of the church. But it's hard to figure out how to communicate that without having some of this data to back it up. That's one of the best ways to be able to advocate for it.

The second one is that there is nothing wrong with curriculum. You're going to use curriculum. That's just sort of an understood part of children's ministry nowadays. But my biggest advocacy for those in children's ministry is do not let your curriculum drive the bus. Curriculum is good. Curriculum is important. I write curriculum. I'm a big fan of curriculum. But a lot of times, we let the curriculum run our children's ministry, and we don't have a bigger vision for what we're really trying to accomplish. No curriculum is going to build intergenerational culture. Curriculum can contribute to building intergenerational culture, but you have to decide for yourself that you want to use it that way.

Even curriculum that is attached to a model of some sort – models don't build intergenerational culture. You have to have that vision. You use things like models and things like curriculum to help you work toward.

I think that's an important thing to highlight. That the curriculum and the models can't create the culture. They can contribute to the culture. I think that's an important highlight. Let the tool serve the carpenter, not the tool be the carpenter.

Exactly. I see, too often, churches that are beholden to whatever curriculum they've invested in. When there's a discussion of, "Oh, we could do an intergenerational such and such this Sunday," and they say, "Oh, nope, we've already got curriculum planned for that Sunday." We feel like we just have to keep going, because we've always done it this way, right?

Right.

Know your stuff, read and study, don't let your curriculum drive the bus, and then my other recommendation, and this is so important when you're on a staff, particularly, but even if you're dealing with a lot of volunteers or if you're a volunteer, you've got to be in relationship with people who are leading other ministry areas. In the same way that we want our children to be engaged with people outside of children's ministry, we can't just have blinders on to focus only on children's ministry. Ministry is still going to be programmatic. Even when we shift out of a program-based mindset, we're still going to have programs. But we have to build the bridges so that our programs begin to connect and our programs begin to contribute to that larger culture.

One of my favorite things that I've heard, actually, a youth minister tell me, was that the children's minister of their church came to her and said, "I want to know what you want the kids to know when they enter youth group, so that I can form my children's ministry curriculum around how we become an on-ramp to then pass them off to you in the youth ministry." That idea of "handoffs" is so important when it comes to children's and youth ministry. That should be a no-brainer, a given, in most churches, and it is often not. So, see yourself in partnership with other ministry areas, particularly youth ministry.

This one's a little bit harder, sometimes, because it may not be how your church is set up, but I think children's ministers have to be involved in worship planning. That Sunday experience, that Sunday morning, that weekend experience. I think most of our churches still consider that to be sort of the "core foundational experience," that foundational gathering time for the church, so being involved in worship planning is essential. One of the things that is just assumed any time I work with a church is we've got to work to get kids in worship. If kids aren't in worship, we're missing the most important piece of building intergenerational culture.

We have to practice those core experiences of the church. Those have to be practiced intergenerationally. Worship is one of the easiest places to do that, if everybody understands what they're trying to do. It's so important that the people who know children best are involved in the worship planning.

Many of you probably are needing to work toward that, rather than that already being the case. Building intergenerational culture needs the people who understand those different constituents. The children's minister needs to be involved with worship planning if children are going to be included in the service.

All right. Before we wrap up – it would almost be the Part B of that question –what about the person who is either in a church where they're the only one on the children's ministry staff or they're simply in a position where they don't really have the authority to make decisions that change the culture? What are the little things that they can do to start changing the culture, I don't know, maybe from the backdoor?

Yeah, I think those are some of them, in some ways, is to ask those questions and to be as proactive as you can be, from where you are, in asking questions. How are children going to be involved in this? How are we connecting the children's ministry to what the mission's ministry is doing? Asking that question of the child's place in everything, cause, if nothing else, a children's minister is a minister to children. But I find just as often the children's minister is an advocate for children.

If you're doing your job well, then you are asking those questions. You are keeping children at the forefront of everything else the church is doing and asking the right questions in that way.

That's part of why I advocate for knowing some of this data and reading some of these books, asking some of those questions, connecting with people who are doing this, because having some of that concrete information helps when you're in those conversations. When you get the opportunity to talk to your senior pastor, to be able to advocate to her or him in that way, because you have data to back it up. It's not just a feeling that you have. It's not just this crazy idea you had. It is literally what research is telling us is the most important thing for the children of our church.

The other thing that I think, practically, you can do, is don't forget adults. You're an advocate for children, but recognize that, if you want to be an advocate for an intergenerational culture, then you can start by including adults, in some way, in what you're already doing. Make your children's ministry an intergenerational culture, even if you can't necessarily make the whole church an intergenerational culture. There's just a lot of different ways to do those small things, and eventually, if you do enough of it, you might actually change the culture over time.

Right. As we're wrapping up, boy, do I … I feel like we have hit the 10% of the iceberg.

That's about right!

Thank you so much, Melissa. I really, really appreciate this.

All right, my pleasure.

Rev. Melissa Cooper

Rev. Melissa Cooper currently serves as the Minister of Worship and Arts at St. Luke's United Methodist Church in Orlando, FL. She also serves as an Associate (coach/consultant) with Vibrant Faith. She is an expert in intergenerational culture-building and is passionate about developing leaders for intergenerational faith communities. She is married to Will, and they're the parents of the cutest poodle you'll ever meet.

BRIAN DOLLAR

How do I get—and stay—creative?

I'm here today with Brian Dollar Thanks for joining me Brian.

I am excited to be with you buddy. Good to see you again.

You too. I'm super excited about this interview on creativity. But before we dive in, give a little bit of background. What's been your ministry journey? What contexts have you served in? Where do you serve now?

Well I've been serving in kids' ministry over 25 years, formally. When I was in junior high in high school I volunteered at my church that I was growing up in. Very small church in Texas. Then when I went to Bible College I started serving as a volunteer in children's ministry. Really it was as the "volunteer" kids' pastor. The former kids' pastor had left, my senior pastor said, hey would you be willing to fill in for a couple of weeks? Well a couple of weeks turned into three years! So that was fun.

Ultimately, through a series of events, God just really revealed to me, "This is what I've been planning for you all along." So I became full time kids' pastor in a church of about 650, 700. I served there eight and a half years. Then God called me about 18 and a half years ago here to a church in North Little Rock, Arkansas and it has grown from, I think we had 200 kids when I first got here to well over 700 kids now. So we're just continuing to serve and loving every minute of it man.

Wow, sounds great. Well...I know that you are passionate about creativity and you've been creating resources for a long time [chuckles]. And that was not an "old joke."

[Laughs] Yeah, just call me one of the geriatric crew.

Exactly! So, a combined question: How do you keep that creative edge? And the flip side of that: What are two or three of those "creativity killers" that keep people from keeping that edge?

Well you know I have to work at it all the time. We started developing High Voltage Kids Ministry Resources about 15 years ago. At first, we were only creating our own stuff, once every three or four months, and I was using some other curriculum. Then my pastor and I in 2005 decided that we were going to have the kids learn the exact same thing as the adults. So he and I started working together on putting series together. We suddenly went from doing one series every three or four months to every week is a full blown, from scratch, all the videos, all the graphics...everything! So, man, you talk about having to put in high gear, we really had to do that.

Now I will tell you at first we weren't that good. [Laughs] We were falling behind. It was just horrible. We were just trying to keep up! But over a period of time we got into a groove and really it all comes down to working ahead. We work way ahead. We're looking at next year. We already have all the series planned for what we're going to do for the next 12 months. They're not all written, but they're all planned and then we're writing 6-8 weeks ahead of time. Shooting video. Everything is done way in advance.

You mentioned "creativity killers." Well, the first one is procrastination. Because let's just be real here, there's kind of an epidemic of procrastination in kids' ministry. We all have to be able to shoot from the hip and be flexible, you know? When the pastor is going 20 minutes over, we've got to immediately come up with something.

[Laughs] That never happens!

Oh...no. [Rolls eyes]

[Still laughing] I'm sure that's only in your context!

All the time, you've got to create something on the fly. Well, we become so good at that and especially if you do children's ministry a long time. You get this tool box and you can fall into the trap of last minute, Saturday night preparation for the next day. Or some people even on Sunday morning.

Dude, so we create an Easter lesson every year, through High Voltage Kids, and I put it out two or three months ahead of time so people can download it, plan for it. Easter's a big day! This year I had 50+ people download it between Good Friday night and Easter Sunday morning! A ton of them on Easter Sunday morning! I mean they didn't even have time to open it up and read it ahead of time. I could have filled it with all kinds of heresy! They wouldn't have known. That's the kind of procrastination that will kill creativity. You're never going to be creative if you're last minute trying to put stuff together.

So we fight against that. When you're always working last minute, that pressure that you're under, you may think, "Oh man, I can think and come up with stuff really fast."

Well it's not your best work, I guarantee you that! You're going to have a hard time being effective if you're last minute.

So a big key to what we do creatively is that we're never doing the preparation phase in a last minute fashion. I don't care who you are. I know we've got people watching who work a full time job, and then they do children's ministry, and you're my heroes, I'll tell you! 'Cause that's huge! But I have some people in that context who tell me, "I can't work ahead because I'm just too busy." I always ask them, "Did you watch your favorite TV show this week? Because if you made time for that, you've got time to study for the children that you're pouring into, and changing their eternity for crying out loud! It's the Gospel of Jesus Christ! It's more important than CSI, or whatever your show is.

So, anyway, we all have the time. But procrastination is a big one, and duplication is another killer. We've worked very hard to not ever duplicate, not only others but ourselves. I think a lot of times in children's ministry, we just plug-and-play. We don't spend any time getting other curriculums. We just take it as it is and teach it, as opposed to saying, "Alright God, how can I tweak this for my kids? What is it in here that I can really emphasize that will apply to their hearts?" Rather than duplicate or procrastinate, I encourage everybody to innovate and to be what I call a "kidminnovator."

I want to hear, how would you define that. I know you even wrote a book – "Kidminnovation." How would you define that term? Since that's going to be something that I'm sure you're going to use throughout the rest of this.

Well a kidminnovator to me is someone who is willing to allow God to give them a fresh idea. It doesn't mean that you have to write everything from scratch like we do. But what it means is you have to say, "I'm not just going to take something and plug it in." I'm going to say, "God give me a God idea that I can develop and use to make an impact in my church. And beyond that – in my community." It's Kidmin and innovator shoved together – kidminnovator. So that's really what it's all about, it's being fresh in your approach. It's being determined not to just duplicate what's out there. Instead, to be somebody who looks to God for fresh ideas and allowing Him to use that natural creativity that we all have.

Okay. Shifting from what a kidminnovator is, to how somebody can become one. What are the actual characteristics people are trying to develop? Speak more to somebody who says, "Okay I'm buying into this, but this has been a struggle for me. The procrastination thing. I want to be more creative. I love my kids' ministry and I want to become a kidminnovator. What's the "how" of that?

Well the how of that is – first of all – kidminnovators question everything! If you're innovating, you're constantly questioning the status quo and what's in front of you. You don't settle for what's always been done, and you don't say "Well that's the way we've always done it."

Those are people who get stale and their ministry gets old, and then kids completely get turned off. A kidminnovator is always questioning their methods, their practices, their strategies. 'Cause you want to make sure that you're taking the best possible approach. So you've got to be willing to question everything in your ministry. Even the things that you think on the outside, you look at it, and you think it's going wonderfully. You say, "I thought the motto I'm supposed to live by is, 'if it ain't broke don't fix it.'" The problem, Keith, is that often when it's something that we came up with and something that we love, a lot of things are broke before we ever get the memo.

If you don't have a habit of questioning the methods and the strategies, you're going to probably be so oblivious that something might be broken, while you're convinced it's never been better. Can I tell a quick story?

Sure.

Several years ago, I kind of began to poke and prod, and question the effectiveness of our Sunday morning kids' experience. Now, you've got to understand, at the time we'd never had more kids than we had! We had kids' pastors from all over the country traveling to our church. Wanting to see what we were doing and learning. If I would have gone by those indicators by themselves, I never would have questioned anything we were doing. But I began to question and evaluate. Without going into all the details, basically I came to the conclusion that our Sunday morning experience was broken. Now, everybody else was convinced that it had never been better. But I knew that it needed a complete overhaul.

So I put together a team of strategists and thinkers to kind of help redesign everything from the ground up. Six months later we launched our new approach and it rocked man! It ended up being the impetus for what we now have as our High Voltage Power Packs. We completely reorganized and changed everything that we've been doing.

But listen, if I hadn't been willing to question what was seeming to be already be going right, I never would have gotten our ministry to that place. So kidminnovators are consummate questioners. You got to question everything. I think sometimes we're not willing to question or evaluate 'cause we're afraid of what we might find. We don't lift the hood of our ministry vehicle, so to speak, 'cause we're afraid we'll see all kinds of deterioration and problems that we just need to fix and we don't have time for that. But we've got to be willing to question everything, if you're going to be as creative and as innovative as you need to be.

Another characteristic is that kidminnovators look everywhere for ideas and inspiration. I'm not talking about duplicating something, but you've got to be open to kid culture and being plugged in to what is hot with kids so that you can find what is capturing their imagination and their attention. The key is always to have your "finder" turned on, and you're always trying to sense is there a lesson here? Is there something I can use here to help bring the Gospel alive for kids?

Now, you know there are some downsides to being a kidminnovator. One of those is that you take more criticism. Innovators take more criticism. I mean you're blazing a trail! You're challenging the status quo, and I'll tell you, I found when I started teaching on this and talking about this, I had a lot of kids' ministry leaders kind of mad at me. Because I was making them uncomfortable. They didn't want to challenge the status quo. They liked the way things were going. They're like, "I don't want to question everything!"

They started taking shots at me because I was willing to stick my neck out and go first. I'll tell you, it's no fun being criticized but criticism is just part of the deal, you know?

Yeah.

If you want to avoid criticism in ministry, don't do anything new! [Laughs] Just copy what's already a success, do what's already been proven to work. You'll never be criticized, but you probably also won't make an eternal difference. I'll give you one more, one more kidminnovator characteristic.

Perfect.

Again, I talked about downsides and this can be looked at as a downside, but kidminnovators, they make more mistakes. The reason why you make more mistakes is 'cause you're trying something that's never been done before. Sometimes we don't do new things because we have this gigantic fear of failure, kind of sitting on our chest like the 900 pound gorilla. It keeps us from moving and doing anything, 'cause we're afraid of making mistakes. You got to realize that failure and mistakes are going to happen. I mean you're going to fail, in that you're either going to fail when you try something new or you'll fail to ever try anything new! I'd much rather be known for the former than the latter.

I think a lot of people look at people who had success in ministry and especially creative people, and they think, "Well, they've never made the mistakes that I have. They've never blown it like I have." Are you kidding me? I mean, I wrote a book called I Blew It! I've made a ton of mistakes! The difference between a kidminnovator and somebody else, is that kidminnovators study their mistakes. They don't just make them. They don't waste a great failure! They study it, they dissect it, and they find out why it happened and where they went wrong. Then they apply what they've learned to their next innovation.

Yeah, you can't get better if you're not willing to risk.

That's right, and you're going to fail…so get used to it. Get rid of that fear of failure and instead, fear is in all of our lives. I think some people think that courage is the absence of fear. But it's not, courage is the willingness to take action in the face of fear, and realizing that our God is bigger than our fears. Our God who is the ultimate Creator and who gives us His unlimited creativity, He's going to be the one that leads us forward.

So you're not depending on your own ideas anyway! Get that fear out of here. You're depending on God's ideas. You're saying, "Holy Spirit, inspire me with an idea that I can develop to minister to the kids that You've called me to minister to." If you're relying on your own thoughts, well, if you fail, that's your fault. But if you're relying on the Lord and you make a mistake, He's going to help you find the nugget of truth that'll get you to the next step. And ultimately, He's going to bring about what He's called you to do.

Piggy backing on that, one thing I noticed when I was doing youth ministry and this certainly applies in the Kidmin space as well, is that most of the mistakes that we make, the kids themselves never notice it. We're frustrated, but they're just in the middle of whatever they're doing and they don't see that this activity didn't work, or this game.

I also find, and this could be another whole chapter in a book on leading well, but I find that the people that are on our teams – whether we're a small church and we only have three volunteers and us, or we have a team of 25 people and we're leading in a large church – that how you, as the leader, embrace and learn from, and handle failure is actually part of your leadership of your team. If they see somebody that's willing to take a risk and handle that failure with grace and humility – and sometimes apology – that actually empowers those leaders to take risks. Frequently that is going to remove some of the burden and unleash their own creativity.

Again, I think we could do a whole chapter on the fear of failure and how shifting our own mindset around that topic can make us better leaders, as well as better volunteers and pastors.

You're exactly right.

As we wrap up, what would you say to the person who's reading this, and says, "Okay that's great but I'm just not wired creatively? I'm just not creative." What would you say?

What I'd say is that anybody who says, "I'm just not creative." I always look at them and I say, "Really? Think back to when you were a child, when you were a kid. You were one of the most creative people around. I mean all you needed was a stick and a cardboard box and you were creating all kinds of things!" I remember when I was a kid if I found one of those cardboard tubes that the paper towels came on.

You mean "swords?" [Laughs]

Exactly! Or it was a microphone, or it was a telescope, or it was whatever. I ask them, and they're like, "Well yeah I remember that." I always follow it up with, "What happened?" I'll tell you what happened. What happens is, as we grow, we become more self-conscious. We're worried about what others think and we allow society to just squeeze that creativity and that innovative spirit out of us. Because that was placed there by God! God is the ultimate Creator. Even the most creative minds are finite. But the term "finite" means having bounds, or limits; it's measurable. But God's not that. He's infinite. He is far above all. He's not limited by any boundaries at all.

So I think the reason why we think we're not creative is because we're thinking about ourselves. We're not thinking about our creative God. We've allowed society to squeeze that out, and we believe that we're just not creative.

But God's power, His love, His plans, they're far beyond anything we could ever imagine. I think if we cultivate that attentive heart, and we're really asking, "God give me a new vision, a new idea."

Listen, we'll never come close to the depths of His greatness, but we can take several steps closer. In Ephesians 3:20, I love what Paul says and I'll read it here. He says, "Now to him who is able to do immeasurably more than all we ask or imagine according to His power that is at work within us." I think that's the key! God's power is what we're leaning on, so forget this idea of "I'm not a creative person." The biggest dream you can imagine about how God could use you in His kingdom is still smaller than what His actual dream for you is.

Absolutely!

I think far too often we forget that the power of God is what is going to inspire us. So forget making excuses, forget talking about how you're not naturally creative and instead open your heart to receive. Ask! Say, "God will You give me an idea that I can cultivate and use to make a giant impact on the eternity of the kids that You've called me to reach?"

I promise if the person reading these words or listening to me right now, if they will just make some time over the next couple of days, set aside some time to just get alone with God. Maybe out in His creation, where it's really easy to be inspired, and see that "Man! I'm serving the ultimate Creator! Then say, "God will You help me to take the leap into the realm of kidminnovation? Will You help me conquer the fear that has held me back from being the innovative leader that You have called me to be?"

I believe that God will do it! And I don't care who you are. You have the creativity, because you serve the ultimate Creator.

Amen. What a perfect place to end. Every time we talk you inspire me, so thank you so much for sharing with us here.

Absolutely man. It was my honor.

Brian Dollar

Brian has served in Kids Ministry since 1992. He founded High Voltage Kids Ministry Resources in 1998, which creates and provides Kids Church Curriculum, Music, Games, Videos, and more to churches around the world. Over 10,000 churches have used High Voltage Kids Ministry materials! He is the author of "I Blew It!", "Kidminnovation", and "Talk Now And Later", a book to help parents lead their kids through life's most difficult topics. Brian and his wife, Cherith, have two amazing children – Ashton and Jordan. He loves running, hiking, and watching his favorite sports teams: the Dallas Mavericks and the Dallas Cowboys.

How do I do effective ministry in a small church?

I'm here today with Bill Gunter, also known as Commander Bill. Thank you so much for joining me today, Bill.

Thanks for having me. It's a pleasure to be here.

I'm excited to talk with you about how we equip the small church and do effective ministry in the small church. First, give us a little bit of context of who you are what your ministry journey has been so far.

I've always served as a volunteer. There's a short time I got a small stipend as a children's pastor. I was raised in a small church and after Bible college went back there and led the children's ministry for a number of years before moving on to what would be called a medium-sized church. That's where I got introduced to Awana and became known as Commander Bill. And that was a ministry of about 100 kids. They then planted a church and I became the children's pastor of that church – which was a small church. During my time there it never got to be more than 100 people. And so, I got the full taste! Had to develop child protection policies and the whole nine yards for children's ministry.

And from there, I've gone to a larger church. I think I'm there to see what a large church is like and the different functions of a large church because I hear about it, but now I've been a part of it. I'm currently still a volunteer. I'm teaching Sunday School. The Awana year just ended. I'm active in VBS. I have just always been a volunteer. And that's my past, my journey that I've taken.

Good. You've already used the word "volunteer" and the phrase "small church" several times. I know that's a passion of yours. And not just a passion but really a burden. For those serving in those contexts, in the small church. Why is that?

It's because I've been there. And with technology and Facebook and being able to connect with other children's pastors in different parts of the country, being able to attend CPC and things of that nature and other national conferences, I've come to see that a lot of times people don't think about the small church.

Here's an example… Every time that I've gone to a conference, it's been on my dime. And working a full-time job, that's my vacation! And so, last year there was a conference that was a destination conference, which means the emphasis wasn't necessarily the conference, it was the location. They started plugging the location. And everybody's talking about, "What are you going to do at this location?" And I'm sitting there thinking "Wait! I'm going for the conference. This is my vacation! My vacation is the conference! And these people, full-time on the church's dime so to speak, they were able to take a day and use that for their vacation.

I posted something on Facebook about how a lot of people volunteer or are sacrificing their time or vacations. And it resonated with a lot of people. And I realized that there's a need. People in a small church kind of feel lonely. They're struggling because they're trying to balance time and different things. Sometimes, even at conferences, I've asked full-time people what advice do you have for the volunteer? And they have nothing. It's not because they're not skilled in what they do, it's because they can't relate. Because of time schedules and things of that nature. They don't understand what it's like when you're at a children's ministry event and that's your vacation.

So they're usually under-resourced, under-funded. They feel like they're serving alone especially in a small church because it may be just you taking care of the children's ministry in a small church with two or three other people. I always hear "Come to this conference and bring your team!" Well, my team is me and my wife. That's the team!

And so, it's trying to network and encourage and support people in a small church because it's so easy to feel left out from church in general that way.

Let's tackle a couple of the most common issues or challenges that people face in serving or volunteering at a small church. And one is the diverse age group that they're teaching. So often in a big church, you've got a 2nd Grade class and a 3rd Grade class and a 4th Grade class. And you go to a small church and it's okay, now we have 1st thru 6th graders in one room and 7th thru 12th graders in another room. How do you teach a diverse age range of children?

With the idea that you have large group and small group, I sit back and say, my large group is my small group! [Laughs] And so, it's tough to differentiate that. But I've been in situations where I've taught kindergarten up through 6th Grade. And it can be a challenge, but it's very doable. Years ago you had the one room schoolhouse. We had the same kind of concept. We had multiple people, different ages being taught in one room at the same time. And the way you handle that in a church situation, especially a small church, is you need to establish respect for the other people in the room. You can't let kids be goofing off all the time, things of that nature. You have to control the room. And when you're teaching, you teach toward the older kids because the younger kids will come up. They are looking up to the older kids. But if you're teaching down to the younger kids, you've lost the older ones because it's way below their level.

Absolutely. I totally agree.

And so, the way you give applications to different things, give an application for each age group so that they can connect to it. And you really need to know the kids you're teaching. I was in a situation once and I referenced the school lunch table. And one kid perks up and says what's a lunch table? We're all homeschooled. I panned to the left and I panned to the right. And they were right. They were all homeschoolers. They had no idea what it was like to sit at a lunch table at school. And so, as you give examples, you have to know the kids that are there. You have to be able to relate to them.

The other key to teaching multiple ages is you have the older kids help out and serve as much as you can. Because as they get to 5th or 6th Grade, they want to head to youth group and so they're kind of checking out. If you can get them connected and serving in some way, that's great. In my case, I used technology. I had them use the same presentation software in the kid's ministry that they used in the adult service, in the main service. What happened was…what they were learning downstairs with the kids they could then transfer those skills upstairs and begin serving upstairs. That kept them engaged.

I do a lot with Awana. And even with Awana, 5th and 6th graders were checking out. I had parents coming to me say "Hey, can they go to youth?" And I said, "This is what I want to propose. They could be a student leader and help out with the younger kids, but they have to be working in their handbooks. And they went along with that because they wanted their kids to serve and their kids had a responsibility. And the younger kids began to look up to the older kids. And so, as they get older, they want to serve. And it begins a whole chain reaction that way.

Good, good. So, we have looked at several different ways we can reach the children. Another huge challenge that people face is that in a small church, you're oftentimes just a team of volunteers or you've got one part-time person who's organizing things. Everybody else is a volunteer. And so, you've got people who are working other jobs. I know you already alluded to that in your answer to that first question about your own journey. You work other jobs and you also volunteer. How do you balance your time where you're working a full-time job while serving ministry in various ways? How do you do that and stay healthy yourself?

The secret is you really can't balance it. Frank Bealer came out with a book, The Myth of Balance. Once you get things balanced and things are kind of okay – "I've got 9-5 job. From 6-8, I'm doing ministry…" – somebody gets sick, the phone rings, something happens. And so, things never quite stay balanced.

The secret really is to prioritize what you're doing. You have to keep focused on work. And I know that when you're in ministry, you're thinking about ministry 24 hours a day. You get an idea, you get a thought, and you say, "Hey, that would be awesome." And so, you find yourself throughout the day jotting down notes in whatever context it is. But, you need boundaries in what you do.

Here is one time I didn't do that well. I found myself last year going to a conference. Driving to a conference, I get an email from a customer. And so, I check with my bosses. My email says I'm not in the office, not checking email. But it's kind of important.

Well, what happened was that week – on my vacation – I ended up putting in two or three days, time-wise, working on jobs to help this customer. I was actually sitting in a breakout, led by a friend of mine, and he was talking about boundaries. I was sitting in the back of the workshop doing work with my laptop open, checking on things from work, while he's talking about keeping boundaries! That wasn't a good week for me because it was my vacation and I was stressing because of work.

In the same way, when you're doing ministry, you can't focus too much on work. It does get muddy! But it's just trying to keep your priorities and know what needs to be worked on. And there will be times you will feel like you're neglecting one or the other. But you just need to do that.

The other thing I struggled with a lot was taking a Sabbath rest. Youtalk to full-time people and they say, "Make sure you get a day you can rest. And that's usually Monday for them. Well, people are working Monday through Friday. Saturday's prep work for ministry. Sunday is ministry. And so, when do you take a break? So, what I try to do is Friday evening. I've become known for "Fire Pit Fridays." I'll sit in the back yard, light a fire, and I'll just sit and relax and not think about work. Not think about ministry. Just spend time with God. Read a book. Go to bed that night. Rest. And then, Saturday morning have a few hours where it's just the same thing. Just relaxing, not focused on work, not focused on ministry, just taking that rest.

It's not a full 24 hours but it's an evening and a morning and it's a time to rejuvenate and rest. And it's important to do that. I can't always do it. It may rain or something. Some things come up. But you do what you can to take that rest. Prioritize what you have.

If you do have a team of other volunteers, try to delegate what you can. Work with the times that people have. And utilize them the best that you can.

Prioritization and boundaries and Sabbath. I've referred to Sabbath as the thing that God takes very, very seriously and Christians do not.

Right.

It's something that is so necessary for both our own health and even the effectiveness of our ministry. We'll simply do better ministry if we spend some time that week not thinking about ministry.

Now we've looked at serving the kids. We've looked at staying healthy. And before we wrap this up, do you have one or two other lessons you've learned from serving in a small church?

Yes. In the small church, you really need to be flexible. You have to plan for 10-12 kids, or 25 kids, whatever number of kids you would normally have…knowing that you may only have four! And not getting discouraged if nobody shows up. Don't get discouraged. Don't take it personally. One night, we had four youth and none of them showed up. And the other youth leader was really bummed out – and I was too somewhat –but it becomes refocusing. One was visiting a Christian college. One was at a rehearsal for an Easter cantata. And the other two were doing similar type things.

And I'm like, if you were in a big church and you lose four people it's not a big deal. But when you've only got four and none of them were there, it can hurt. But what else would you rather them doing? They are doing things for God or checking things out for their future, a Christian life. And that's what you want.

But you have to be ready. If you expect nobody… One time, we didn't expect any kids to be there. And two visitors showed up!

Another time, we had a summer camp working with other churches. It was a weekly thing. And so, we had people set up to take care of whoever might show up for that midweek activity, not knowing if anybody was going to show up! But I had leaders, other volunteers there, ready to minister to whoever showed up. One night, one family showed. And another random night there were 20 kids there. And so, you have to be ready for whatever number show up.

Another lesson: Don't covet. Don't be looking at the church down the street and say, "If we had more kids…or if we had more money…or if we had more volunteers…" So often we focus on numbers. But in a small church, you can really reach out to the kids and have an impact because you're building a deep relationship. And so, you need to focus on that. Don't get caught up with numbers. Just focus on who's there and minister to them.

And the last thing that really helped me was…I used to sit there and think, "Why don't other people have the same passion I have to reach kids?" But in a small church, you're probably the only one. And I realized: "If other people had the same passion I had, they'd be in my position!" So, you want other people coming along beside of you growing that passion, a desire to reach kids. But they may not already have the same passion you have. You just work with them and you do what God's called you to do. You keep that focus on what God wants you to do. And who he wants you to be.

Wow, that's great. Thank you so much. Looking at how to serve multiple ranges and ages of kids and balancing or prioritizing. And boundaries and Sabbath so you can serve for the long haul. And flexibility. I relate to so much to what you said here because I've had the times of no kids, or two kids, showing up to youth group. I love the idea of remembering that you can actually go deeper many times in a smaller church. You can connect with those kids. And you want to always communicate to those kids just how valuable they are. And sometimes, the small church is absolutely the best place to do that.

Thank you so much for taking your time today, Bill.

Thanks. I enjoy helping out small churches.

Bill Gunter

Bill is the founder of SmallChurchKidMin.com where he seeks to encourage and support the many serving in children's ministry in a small church. He currently serves as a Children's Pastor in a small church and has served as a volunteer in several areas and churches. He has over 30 years of ministry experience and is known as "Commander Bill" as he maintains an Awana and Children's Ministry resource site at CommanderBill.net.

How do I engage the whole family?

I'm here with Dawn Heckert. Thank you so much for joining me.

I'm glad to be with you today.

So, tell us before we dive in, tell us a little bit about your ministry journey and what context you serve in now.

I've been at Children's Ministry for the last 15 years. I spent ten years in an Anglican church, and then I decided to shift to an EVFree church. They're dramatically different in many ways, but it also shifted from a single campus to a multi-site campus. I'm at the largest of the multi-sites. I have about 250 kids who are underneath my ministry, and I serve with a team of children's ministries across those five campuses, collectively sharing our ideas and focusing on families in different ways.

That's great. I've had the privilege of seeing you in both of those contexts, so it's been fun to see those differences...and you enjoying both! Now looking at engaging families and different ways to engage them, there's something that we need to clear up. [Laughs] You have sometimes been called a "Ministry Killer." I know this actually ties into this topic, so I want you to unpack a little bit of how you got that moniker, what it really means, and why you actually like it!

First off, I am the friendliest person you will ever meet, Keith! [Laughs]

[Laughing] I know, I know.

But, I really think that, when it comes to ministry…[Pauses] When I first started in ministry, I was following a leader and following the patterns that had been in ministry before me. I just remember one day, I was walking through the area of the Children's Ministry and I was praying. I said, "God, what do you want to do here, and what am I not doing for you?" And it was as though he just said, "You're doing everything you want, but nothing that I'm asking you to do."

That began a season to re-examine my ministry and what my philosophy was. What ministry was going to be. And once that was in place, Keith, I became the "Ministry Killer." I began eliminating programs that didn't focus on family. I felt like God had taken me from thinking just children's ministry, into thinking family ministry.

He was saying to me, "You've been focused on a third of the family, a fourth of the family, or two-fourths of the family. But I want you to focus on the whole thing. I want 100% family." And that meant a lot of things that I was doing had to go by the wayside. At both my churches, I have made really hard decisions to let some things go that have been part of tradition in the church for a long time, for the better, for the thing that I feel like God has led me to. And I will tell you, at every turn when I have made those choices, as hard as they've been emotionally, mentally, spiritually with other leaders to make those choices, He has blessed them tenfold.

Staying here for just a second…We didn't even talk about discussing this, but as you mention making these hard decisions, you mentioned walking through the childrens' ministry area, and praying, and feeling God saying something. It seems like, if you're going to make those hard decisions, your own conversations with God better be frequent and authentic. A regular part of your life if you are going to be able to make those decisions with any kind of boldness or confidence whatsoever.

I was in that kind of season, Keith, when I realized when God was responding to me, "You've been doing everything you've wanted, but not what I've asked." I was so stunned to silence. I mean it was as though God just clamped my mouth and said, "You're going to sit and you're going to listen, and sometimes you're going to listen for silence because you're going to want to get up and do something. And I don't want you to do anything right now."

Because I was a doer. I am a doer. I love people. I love serving people. And He was breaking a part of a nature inside of me that had been there since I was a child to go meet people's needs, and I needed to meet His needs for His people. And so, I was in a great, deep season. I would almost tell you it felt like a pit of despair sometimes, because He wasn't giving me a task. He wasn't giving me anything other than Him and being with Him.

That was a really hard season. It lasted almost five years before I felt like He brought me to a place and into relationships with other people who were feeling the same heartache and pain that I was. That I was only catching a smidge of what God wanted, and He wanted it all. And He said, "I'm here for my families." In Psalm 78 it says that families will talk about this and it will be passed down from generation to generation. I wasn't giving anything to pass down from generation to generation because I wasn't giving families enough. And so that was a hard season for me, and it remains that way. When I wait on the Lord I often tell people, "I just need you to pray. I don't want to pull out an old bag of tricks, I don't want to pull out things that are easy and simple for me, I want to move where the Spirit is moving and go where God is leading. And that means we all have to be better listeners, and we have to trust that inkling inside of us that says, 'This is go time.' Even if we don't 100% know what 'go time' looks like, we're in. We're going!" So, it's thrilling and hard at the same time.

Oh yes. Yes. And when those hard decisions are made, you're going to have people who don't buy in right away. I would imagine that having that level of, I'm going to call it "intimacy with God," would give you the confidence and boldness to say, "Hey but this is what God's calling me to do, and I can weather this storm."

Honestly, Keith, I had to get to a point where I really submit myself to say, "This is not my battle to win. If this is where God is moving, He's going to clear the path of the disheartened or the disenchanted with me." It's not about me. It's about Him and where He wants to go. And there have been may times where I've sat in on hard conversations with people who do not like me per se, because I'm changing, I'm "moving the cheese" of their ministry, what they've done for years in places. And yet when they're done, and we're moving in the right way, they often come back and say, "Oh my gosh, this is so much better! I couldn't see it. I had blinders on and your eyes were open." And so it's been really hard. It's not an easy thing. Ministry Killer is a really hard title.

I bet! So, we've looked at this "mindset" piece and the "heart" piece of making these decisions. The way you and I have talked about that playing out practically is, you've identified these "milestone moments" that you've now tried to build some things around, so tell us about "milestone moments" and how you thought through that and put it into play.

In those hard, intimate moments with God, He developed a philosophy in my heart for what family look like. And the reality is, family is messy. They're naïve sometimes, or they're overzealous and they think they know it all. And so you're working with lots of different types of people. And as I began to re-examine the ministry, we looked at milestone moments and we said, "We want to create spots where we're intersecting in the lives of our families at very strategic times." And it used to be that the church just said, "This is the strategic time. This is what we're doing." And that was one of the things I kind of had to come in to kill and say, "No this isn't about the church. This is about the child in this very strategic moment. And the person they're with the most is their parents!" So how do we come alongside this child and the parents and take a back seat and deliver what they need?

And so we have four milestones we began to re-examine. They were Child Dedication, when a family first comes to our church and says, "We need your help raising this child to know and love and serve the Lord, and choose Him one day for their own." We have 1st Grade Bible Moments. As children are becoming readers, you're no longer just telling the story, but they're becoming seekers of the story. They're learning to read words, and we want to give them a simple Bible that would engage them. But how do we do that as a church, not just giving them a Bible, but making that a family moment? That was something we were going to change. Our 5th graders receive a Bible that takes them out of that early child reader kind of version, and into the kind of Bible that our church is using in worship service. So when they're attenders upstairs and worship, when we do worship together as families, they are in the same Good Book that their parents, and everyone sitting next to them, are in.

And then finally, Baptism is sometimes part of your ministry choice for kids. As they grow through these elementary years, how do we help parents to just talk about baptism with the kids and for their kids to choose that?

So, when we look back at the first one it's the easiest one. When we did child dedication it used to be the church would say, "Come up here. We're receiving you. Name your child. What's your name?" And the parents would say their names, they'd name their kid, and then you would see a pastor pray blessing over that kid and bless the kid, and that was it. It was the church driving that moment. Now we teach a class on child dedication that we encourage parents to understand, "How do I bless my child?" What does blessing mean in the Bible? Where is that found? How does altering the words I speak over my child change their day and the environment that I set them up for?

And so we teach them how to write a blessing for their children and we say to them, "You are who God is going to speak through, and to, always about this child. Even before the church, it's you. And so we want to help you cultivate language around that." And so they will write that blessing. And now, in that service moment, the families stand up; they introduce themselves, they introduce the child that God has given them, and they speak the blessing they have found for their child over them. And it's far more intimate for everyone sitting in the church because we get to know a family and their child that the words God's gifted them in that season. And we hang those up. Those blessings and those children's photos in our children's area, in the nursery, in the toddler rooms, so that our workers are now speaking the words the family has chosen over that child, over and over again. So we take it into very practical ways of how to keep doing that and we encourage parents to do that.

As they move into their 1st Grade Bibles, it was the same thing. We often chose the Bible. We gave it to the child and we said, "Here's your 1st Grade Moment." It was like doing a parade of families, which was awful! It was like, "Hey these are the people that you don't ever meet that live downstairs." You know. "They're in your neighborhood but you don't know them." And we were just spotlighting them in that moment. So instead, we created a space where we bring parents in, we talk about the value of what reading is going to mean. It's going to open their eyes and it's going to lead them to new intimacy and character of who God is. And how do you do that from scripture with your child?

We still purchase the Bible, but we gift that Bible to the parents weeks before this event. And we say to them, "We want you to write how scripture changed your life, when you discovered the Word of God to your child, and by other people who are going to be influencing your child's life to write messages in those Bibles to highlight passages that are important to them." And then now parents stand up, introduce their child, and they tell a scripture that they feel God has laid on their heart for their child to know and that it's in there, it's highlighted for them. So now, again, the parents are leading that moment in the church, and people are hearing. "Oh I recognize that verse! That's a powerful verse in my life. I can go up to that family and connect with them about that verse."

And that kind of mimics our 5th Grade, but the 5th graders are receiving a Bible that's more commonly used. But it's saying to kids, "It's not anymore about just knowing the big story, it's about finding God in these moments, and how He is drawing you out to mimic Him in His character, and what He has for you and the plans He has for you." So it's a more mature version of the Bible and we, again, encourage parents to do the writing in that Bible, to present that Bible to their kids. Those are big moments in our church.

Oh yeah definitely.

Because the parents are starting to hand that Bible to the kids. The kids are ready to crack them open and see, "What have you given me that reminds me that you, my parent, know God through these words too?" I mean it is intimate for them. With our baptisms, what we discovered was, having a class at the church where there are 13 kids sitting around with a children's pastor asking them questions where every kid knows the right answer, "Jesus. Jesus. God. Jesus." You know, that wasn't the intimate moment that we see in scripture! Like when Jesus is going to John the Baptist and saying, "You're going to baptize me. Here's why you're going to baptize me." Or Phillip with the eunuch. Those were intimate moments!

So we decided to create intimate moments. We show up in the family's home when they say, "Our child is starting to talk about this and wants to have that conversation." And we say, "What have the conversations been like already in your home. We want to come alongside you."

So when we show up, we show up for dinner. We break bread with this family and we ask them questions. We start with something easy like, "Hey if you could go back in time, what is the Bible story that you would want to be present for?" And we ask that of the whole family. We share those stories, and we find out, what their knowledge of scripture is. And then we talk about: What does baptism mean to you? What do you think it means?

And then we encourage parents to tell their baptism stories. And we talk about what discipleship looks like out of baptism. This isn't the be-all-end-all. This is the beginning of intimacy and mentorship. And so instead of doing that in a church setting, we've done it in a home setting, because what it says then is, "We value the family as a primary place of discipleship. I'm not the church leader asking your kid, 'What's the right answer?,' and getting 'Jesus.' I'm saying to them, "What story have you found so fascinating you wish you could go back and see God in action?"

So we're taking it out of the church being the driving machine, and making the house or the parents the drivers in this relationship with God.

I love that idea of Milestone Moments. For any given church there might be four – the same four – and there may be ten. There might be six. But I love that idea of, "How do we think about shifting from a church-centric model to a family-centric model?

I know we just have a few minutes left, but what are a couple different examples of what you do differently even on a weekly or annual basis. Some big changes that aren't just Milestone Moments, but even programmatically, some things you've done differently.

This is probably going to be the hardest for your readers to comprehend but we, the ministry killers, even killed VBS! [Gasp!] I killed VBS because lots of times the intentionality was simply around the children. And while I don't think that VBS is a bad thing…I think it's great to put children in the Word! But for me, as I sat and listened to God, He was asking for the whole package, the whole family. Whether it's a mom only with her kids, or a father only with his kids because he's divorced, or it's grandparents with the grandkids because the parents don't have faith, He was asking me to create something that could engage a family. And so we quit doing VBS. We prayed about it for a year, and we came back from that year and we said, "God's inviting us to spend a week with our families modeling how to tell His story. Modeling to families, "How do I talk about that story and make it not about the past, but the present?"

[Modeling a parent saying…] "The fact that God is powerful from today's story could have been part of my week this week. That I needed strength. And it wasn't through my own strength. It was through God's strength, that He was showing up."

And a parent being able to articulate that. Or a kid tell a parent what that looked like.

We have mentor families that come alongside them who have been doing this and can cultivate that. And so for us, one of the first things we did was take away things that were just simply saying, "We're going to pull your child separate from you" and say, "We don't do any of that anymore."

So we don't do that for VBS and we do families only. We also don't do midweek. We aren't going to pull your child away and say, "We're going to teach them something over here that you have no idea what they're learning. And maybe you need to know it and maybe you don't." But rather, we value teaching you all the same thing.

And so, one thing that we've started doing is, for each of the age groups in our ministry, we have "Embraced the Phase" nights. And those are evenings where we say to parents, "We're going to provide child care for all the kids except for this one. This 2nd grader and you are going to get to have a special night tonight. We're going to teach you how to communicate with the 2nd grader on the 2nd grader's level, and how to enjoy who God's created them to be at their level." And those look different. A 2nd or 3rd grader, just so you know Keith, you might know this from your own kids, are all about "competitive play." I mean, if you want a 2nd or 3rd grader to really do something, you should make a game out of it! And so we create these game kind of nights where we're training parents about just who God created their kids to be, and introducing God into those moments in the fun of that 1st, 2nd or 3rd grader.

With our infants, we know communication is huge. God wants our children to trust us, and in an infant, how do you explain trust other than through touch? So we hired a massage therapist to come in and teach parents, "Communication comes through touch and cuddling and oohs and ahs" to their kids. And so we are trying to teach intimacy through communicational phases with our kids, and level those up year after year in little bitty ways. That's really different because it used to be you just drop off your kids and you're like, "What did you learn?" And it's on a piece of paper that ends up in the bottom of your car! But instead, we're saying, "Come, explore that with them, and let us resource you for your week with those details."

I love this. I hear you starting out this conversation talking about the heart and mindset shift that had to happen, and then looking at what it takes to create both events, and language, and structure around these Milestone Moments, and then even being willing to kill something as sacred as VBS or a midweek thing. You've used the word "season" several times throughout this interview. And that there are seasons where you're talking about: the season where you're praying through something, and you've talked about a five-year season, you talk about a one-year season. The thought that comes into my mind is, that somebody reading this doesn't need to, starting next quarter, have all of these things in place: Their heart and mind is shifted. They've got their milestones laid out, and how they're going to act on that. And they're figuring out exactly what they're going to do with the second week of July next year.

I think the starting of the conversation maybe opening up a season that lasts a few months, or a few years, and being comfortable with that. I thought of a phrase that I use all the time: God is not asking you to do everything. He's asking you to do the next right thing.

Exactly.

And that came to my mind so many times as I heard both your heart in it, as well as the practical what you do programmatically. So thank you so much for taking the time. This has been fantastic!

Thank you Keith.

Dawn Heckert

Dawn Heckert is the Children's Pastor at Christ Community Leawood Campus in Leawood, Kansas. She loves Jesus and the opportunity to share his story with all ages. She spends her free time deep in glitter, crafting, creating, and chasing life with her two daughters and husband.

How do I take advantage of the current trends in family ministry?

All right. Today I'm here with Heidi Hensley. Thank you so much for taking the time to be here today.

Yeah, thanks for having me.

Before we dive into some of the trends you're seeing in the church today, give us a bit of an overview of your children's ministry journey thus far and what context you serve in now.

My children's ministry journey has been roughly about 23 years for me. I started in the context of a senior pastor's wife and started doing children's ministry as a necessity. We found ourselves at this little country church that had nothing for kids, and kids in the sanctuary. So of course, I started teaching. I had been mentored as a teenager, as far as teaching Sunday school and different things like that, so I knew what children's ministry was. I didn't have kids myself yet, and I began out of necessity and started at a church where we had three kids in our children's ministry. Over the course of time, that grew.

Ten years into it, we had been at three different churches where we had revitalized them for the denomination we were with, and then eventually landing me at a church where we were in that middle range of 300-500 kids a weekend.

Now I'm in San Diego. I'm the kids director at Shadow Mountain Community Church and absolutely love it. We are a larger church, and so I've got a staff. It's funny. I will use lessons that I learned with three kids in the room when I have a thousand kids a weekend, and it has been a step-by-step journey of God really just teaching me the groundwork and giving me the tools I need to do ministry. The mission or calling has stayed the same. I whole-heartedly believe I am called to teach kids that they can have their own personal relationship with Christ. That's really my driving force of what I do.

All right. So, quite a varied journey. I think that length-of-time-wise, we're both in it about the same. My ministry started 23 years ago as well.

You and I talked about the current trends we're seeing in parents and the kids that we minister to Share with us a little bit about what you're seeing as current trends.

As ministry leaders, we have seen lots of trends about how we minister to the child, how we minister to the family. In the '80s, we were all in our separate spaces in separate youth groups, and then we get into this more recent space. We see the trend is family ministry, and the concepts of family ministry are a beautiful thing. The fact that we minister to families as a whole… We're leaning heavier on the parents for the spiritual guidance of their children, and that's something I love.

One of the things we're seeing and waking up to is the fact that when we use the Deuteronomy 6 model that says, "I'm going to walk along the road as a family. I'm going to talk about these things when I lie down, when I wake up, all these things, with my children and my family in the home," we give these tools to parents, expecting that they're coming knowing how to use them.

What we're not realizing is there's a gap in generations where nobody was doing that, and those people are now our parents. Those are the people who are showing up to church, and we're going, "Here's a flyer. Here's this. Here's communion. Here's baptism. Go teach your kids about that." We give them the information, but nobody's ever taught them!

We're seeing this trend of parents who almost, in a sense, have to be trained up along with their children. They're either coming back to church and haven't been in many, many years, or they're brand new to faith or new believers, or they never even stepped foot in a church and the Christian language just doesn't resonate with them. I truly believe it is a different method of how we minister. I'm finding that we are needing to take a different position along that road that is now culturally relevant, just like it was then, when you had many generations growing up in a house together.

Definitely. The culture is certainly changing massively, so we could go off on a whole lot of different conversations I've had with my high schooler and my middle about how different everything is. And definitely in the church as well.

When you are ministering to these kids and these families, because you've got them side by side, right? You've got these core families that have grown up in the church. They know church They speak the church language. They know it. And you've got these new believers or people returning to church or people that have just simply ... maybe have been in church but haven't been equipped within that. You've got both groups. How can we minister to both that core family as well as the parents who are either new believers or returning to church?

Yeah. One of the things that we know is that kids – regardless of their age – they're still relatively new to faith. Because they haven't been on the earth that long! Regardless, they're "starting." So the ability to dive deep with these kids isn't there.

For the past probably eight to 10 years, we've had this heavy focus on the parents. "Let's build it deep for the parents, so the parents get really pulled in. Then they can translate it to their kids."

The beautiful thing is the Gospel is simple. The words of Jesus are easy to understand. It's us who brings complication to them. I truly believe that. And so by putting more of a focus on the kid [pauses] and I don't want to go as far as saying that we've lost the kid in kids ministry, but to some degree I think we have when we focus primarily on a family ministry. They need to go hand-in-hand. They're one and the same, and so the ability to bring the kid back into kid ministry brings it to a level that a mom can grasp.

For example, I had a mom in our ministry that stepped in, and she came to me one Sunday. There had been some pretty big, significant things that happened in her home, but this visit was caused by the fact that she could not find in the Bible where her child's memory verse was. It was that moment that I realized this woman has never been shown how to use a Bible, and I'm sending her a take-home with small group questions. She's not even sure if this thing I'm telling her about Noah is real.

Right.

That actually happened! When we wake up to those moments in leadership, you realize, "Oh, gosh. I have missed something here. I'm running 12 steps ahead of everybody I'm supposed to be leading."

I stopped. I paused. And we learned that by shooting at the target that was the median age of the child in our ministry, we were going to hit our mark every time. What that meant was instead of sending something home that explained communion, we first backed up and sent something home, so that a child understood what ordinances were. Then they could understand what communion was. And all of these backtracked moments happened. Then we sent something home inviting them to take their kids to service with them and partake in communion as a family if they would choose.

It's just those moments that you're very intentional about what you know, what you believe, and then the practice of it.

The biggest key that I have learned is never to assume that anyone knows what I mean. It's been a huge marker for me in ministry. It affects how I do publicity. It affects how I teach. So, I never assume anybody knows what I mean.

By doing that, I will often hear in feedback from a parent meeting that a core family thanked me for being reminded of a "basic." Something they knew but it's brought new life to it. A new family felt like they were part of the conversation, because it was new to them and it's at their level. They didn't have to lean over and ask, "What does she mean by this? What does that mean? Where do I find this?" By aiming at the child in children's ministry, which sounds ironic, we can instantly pull both core and new families together.

As far as ministry is concerned, like practical steps of how to do this, this has turned into making sure my take-home is no longer small group questions. My take-home is a memory verse, and it actually lists, "Is it in the New Testament or the Old Testament?" That sounds silly, but after seeing what I saw, it's not. We give instructions on how to do a memory verse at home. We give three questions that are life application. We all know that life application can be done by just about everybody, wherever they are in their spiritual walk. So, the meat of the Word, the life application of the Word, and then we actually write out a prayer.

One of the things that we discovered, at least in many of our core families, they pray with their kids when they eat, and they pray with their kids when they go to bed. There's usually not a whole lot of prayer that is not centered around those two things.

Core families wanted to know more about praying with their kids, and people who were new to faith or new to the church, they just needed to be instructed from the beginning. Either way, again, we're hitting right in the middle of that mark by spelling out a prayer. Maybe the prayer is, "Hey, families. This week we want you to pray in your car on the way to school. Simple as that. If you're on a bus, if you're in a car, whatever. It doesn't matter, you can pray together."

Then we actually write out the prayer. Again, families might use it, or they might be a core family who goes, "This is a great idea, but let's just say our prayer." A new mom, who doesn't know what to say and she doesn't know where to start, prayer can be intimidating, especially for a new person in faith. The reality is when you're hitting a new family in faith, you have a parent and a child, but in all actuality, they are the same age as far as spiritual development. We can't just assume that because they're an adult, they instantly understand theology and the deeper meat of Scripture. By starting there, someone who is naturally more mature in their faith is going to take that as a starting point, and they're going to expand on what they know. Someone who's new to faith is now equipped to do exactly what that core family is doing, so it's a very practical step.

The other piece that we do is we offer community moments where our core families, they can come together and actually mentor our new families. Those look as simple as Family Olympics. It's an outreach event that anybody can come to, but we pair core families with new families and get them in. Letting them see how they interact with their kids, how discipline moments happen, how respect happens, leading in prayer. The "Sword Drill" was actually one of our Olympic events, so allowing them to see what that could look like. Those community moments where the Bible tells us constantly to surround ourselves with other believers, because we grow from them. We get sharper by them, and that's true in parenting as well.

As I was listening to you unpack that, the two thoughts that came into my head were: each one of these steps, whether it be the memory verse or talking to the median age – or any of the others – were around the intentionality of what we do to make sure we're serving somebody. A lot of times, we get into this, "Well, this is how we do things every week," or, "This is just the routine that we're in." Or, we just haven't paused long enough to know that we need to be intentional to serve somebody who's in a different context. I think that some of the aha moments you mentioned, like the mom that asked the question about Noah, it takes that sometimes to remind us of the need for intentionality.

The other thought, looking at some of the practical examples that you gave, I found myself thinking the beauty of that these work for a church that has a children's ministry of 20 kids and a church that has a children's ministry of 200 kids. While the scale they're implementing it is different, what they're actually doing – a Bible verse with a few questions or a written prayer – can go home to three families or it can go home to 3,000 families.

Absolutely.

I love that it's completely scalable. Now one follow-up question before we wrap this up. We've talked about ministering to the core family and ministering to a family where the parents are either new believers, returning to church, or something different. But there's this third group of kids that we need to minister to, which is a ... quite honestly, sadly ... a growing group of kids. This is the child that maybe is interested or coming with a friend but has zero spiritual support. Can you just touch on that for a second? What do we do about this kid who's got no support at home spiritually?

Yeah, going back to your core families and your new families, when Deuteronomy talks about walking on that road, the change in how I've done ministry is I don't send them on a road. I walk it with them. The beauty of that is I'm already on the road now, and so if I've got kids in my ministry who have no spiritual support, the ability to either pair them or partner them with another child, another adult who can touch base and just check on them, making sure community is happening. What that looks like on a practical sense is it looks like ... That prayer at the base of that paper was for two reasons. One, it was for that mom who didn't know how to pray, but the second reason was a little boy named Micah that was in my ministry, lived in the projects across the street, and he would come over.

My favorite part of my day is – he called me Miss Lady – and so he would tell me, "Miss Lady, I don't know how I'm supposed to pray." He told me how he was praying, and he had no idea what prayer was. I sat down with him, and I explained what prayer was. I started writing it out for him, and he would come back. He would tell me, "Okay, I've memorized this one. I need a new one." [Both laughing.]

So…all this confusion. It's these things we take for granted. His mom was addicted to meth. She was either out or asleep most of the time. So this kid is walking this road by himself. Again, hitting that middle of the mark where a child can do this without the parental support is going to equip the new parent, the core parent, but it's also going to equip that child who doesn't have the ability to do it himself.

Then the other piece of that is in your programming. It's amazing how we don't really give much merit to the effect of intentional programming. Micah was the child who taught me that behavior modification is not how you teach to have a relationship with Christ. Micah began to understand that he could earn things, and so instead of that, we started focusing on intentionality and heart. When he came in, he had a buddy. The kids in our ministry were supposed to recite their memory verse at home. Micah didn't have anybody who was going to listen to that! So we had kids in our ministry, often those core kids (but not always) that they were just a little bit ahead. They were the kids that they're too smart to sit still. Those ones. [Laughs] Those are the kids that find themselves in the tech booth and doing different things. Cash in on those kids. Give them a sheet of stickers, and let them start quizzing their peers that don't have spiritual support at home.

Micah would come in, and he would find Mark every single week. He would tell Mark his memory verse. It was this moment of celebration, and Mark got excited that he got to be part of it. Micah got excited that he had someone now who was pairing with him. It turned into conversations. It turned into a friendship, and it turned into community.

At the end of the day, the church was the parent walking on the road with this child, and as kids' pastors, it we try to do all of that ourselves, we're only going to minister to ten kids. That's as wide as your arms can go! Empowering the young people in your ministry and the leaders around you, for us, we have seen huge transformation in the kids who come on their own. It's a very practical step. It's free, and it's just intentional programming that builds community in your space.

Boy, that's a great place to end. Intentional programming for community. There's a whole book, more than just this interview in that whole thing, marrying those two concepts right there. Maybe that's going to be our follow-up together.

There you go.

All right. Thanks so much for taking the time, Heidi. I really, really appreciate it.

Yeah, thanks for having me.

Heidi Hensley

Heidi has been in full time ministry since 1995. She is passionate about leadership and ministry that helps kids understand how to own their faith, and constantly raising up a new generation of leaders who love children's ministry as much as she does. Heidi has a Master's Degree from Southern California Seminary, and lives in San Diego with her husband and two (almost) grown sons. Heidi loves the ocean and can be found surfing with her kids on her day off.

How do I recruit and retain volunteers?

I am sitting here today with Steven Knight from Texas.

Hi.

How are you doing, Steven?

I'm doing well. How are you?

Good. Thanks for taking the time.

Yeah, thank you.

Before we dive into talking about recruiting, retaining, and really celebrating volunteers, give us a little bit of your background. Who you are. What's been your ministry journey, and what context do you serve in now?

I've been involved in ministry, different types of roles, for probably close to 15 years now. Heavy involvement in kid's ministry, some involvement with student ministry, and in different church sizes, too. Spent some time working in a church plant, at two larger churches, and at a multi-site church. Now, I serve as the Family Life Pastor at Fellowship Bible Church in Waco, Texas.

So, in my role, I oversee birth up through college, and then ministry to parents as well. So, it's an exciting thing. I get to work with some different ages, heavily involved with our kid's ministry team. I love to work alongside them there, and just for perspective as we're thinking about it, our church size is about 700 right now. I love what I do working with kids and families. It's pretty great.

Now you're also doing children's ministry in your own home as of the last few years.

Oh, yes. Oh, yes. We got two little ones at home. They're great.

Yeah. So, hopefully you won't nod off during the interview!

Hopefully not. Hopefully not. That would be bad.

We're focusing today on volunteers, and before diving into the practical pieces... what does the Bible say? I know we've shared our passion for the Bible over barbecue together, and so what does the Bible say about volunteers?

Well, a few quick thoughts. One, when you look at Ephesians 4, kind of a quick takeaway from a passage in there is thinking about how we're equipping the saints. So, if you're a pastor, director, whatever your title might be in the church, a big part of your role is really equipping the rest of the body of Christ for that work. So, when you think of volunteers, my mind immediately jumps to that Ephesians 4 concept of equipping them to do the work of ministry.

And I also think about 1 Corinthians 12. You can think of the body and the different parts. That's also an important thing, too, to think of. We've got volunteers who we are equipping, but also we have volunteers that are gifted in certain ways to do different things within the body. So, it's an exciting thing to be thinking about – we get the privilege of equipping them for ministry.

Yes. Okay, so, moving on to tips and strategies. So, we're going to break this up into three pieces. We're going to first focus on that initial piece, the recruiting. What are your tips and strategies for recruiting volunteers?

A few thoughts on that. One, when I think about recruiting, I always think about how can we prepare before we start? And sometimes we're not prepared when we go to start recruiting. So, I might even encourage anyone that's in kid's ministry to take an afternoon, get an hour or two away. Do something just to get some alone time, and really think about where your ministry's at. Sit down, maybe write out a big list of…If I were to dream the next two, three, five years, what type of positions would I have on my ministry team? Think of all those different volunteer positions, and just dream a little bit.

Now, the top of your list is probably going to be some positions that are more urgent. Maybe you'd like them today. Maybe you needed them months ago. I totally get that, right? A lot of us are in the same boat of like, "Oh, man we need some help right away!" But just take a moment to think a little bit bigger than that. Write some of those out.

And then once you've spent a little bit of time doing that, I encourage you to look through that list. There are going to be some of the positions that are more urgent, like, "Hey I need someone to teach a certain age group on Sunday." That's really important, but then also just highlight a few things. You're like, "I think this is important in the next year or two. I think this would be important to start looking for this." And from that list, you kind of have somewhere to start as you're thinking about, okay, when I'm asking people, when I'm recruiting for these volunteer positions, this is how I'm going to go about it. Because I kind of know what my needs are then. What the serving opportunities are.

As you get to thinking about preparing to recruit, a few short things. Have you ever heard of a position profile? It's kind of like a job description for a volunteer. Have a description written out. What are you asking people to sign up for and do? I like to bring absolute clarity, because sometimes it's like there's this curtain between you and your potential volunteer that you want to recruit, right? And they have no idea what's behind the curtain.

They've heard of kid's ministry. Kids run around. They're crazy. If you put sugar in them, they're even more crazy! They just don't have that understanding of what's there. And anything you can do to start to pull back that curtain a little bit will help. I think then you start to have clarity. One of those aspects is having a position profile that describes what they would be doing. What that commitment might look like.

I encourage you to do that. Also look at your application process. You've got an interview process in place, and that will look different at every church, of course, but what does that look like? And probably one thing I'd say, too, is assess where your ministry's at so that you can make sure, "Hey is this a healthy place? Are we ready for more people to join the team?"

From there, one of my tips about when you're doing it, is when you're casting vision, you want to have that nailed down. Think, if you're going to have 30 seconds with someone, what do you say? What is that exciting thing that you're going to share about the kid's ministry, or about the serving opportunity.

You know what I mean, Keith? What's that exciting thing you can share that kind of helps motivate people, and they say, "You know what? I can be part of that. I'd love to be a part of that! Something bigger than myself." That's what we'd all love to be a part of – something bigger than ourselves.

So, it's the WHY behind the WHAT.

Exactly. Yep. Yep. Exactly. That's good. And just as you're thinking about that, one of the things that I've talked with a lot of kid's ministry leaders about. We're kind of nervous to make the ask, right? That invite to serve and to volunteer. You can be a little bit nervous, especially if you're newer to it. A few people are naturals, but for most people it takes a little bit of work. So, I want to encourage you. If you're new to it, it will come with time. It's just we want to practice that as much as we can, and continue to improve with that.

But when you think of that ask, you really don't want to focus on the negative. You want to focus on the positive. I'll give you an example of this. If you're nervous to make the ask, a bad example might be, "I know you're really, really busy, but we kind of need help in kid's ministry. We're drowning over here. Can you maybe serve like once a month? I know you're really busy, so just say 'no' if you can't, but could you help us out this way?"

And it sounds funny, right, but I've actually heard kid's ministry leaders make that type of ask before, and I just want to encourage you, focus on the positive. Cast that vision and motivate them. Say, "Hey, we've got an exciting opportunity to invest in the lives of our kids in our kid's ministry, and we'd love to invite you to be a part of that. Maybe you could join the team. Maybe you're serving weekly. Maybe you could serve every other week, but we'd love to just talk with you, and just explore that a little bit more."

And you kind of see the difference there of just how that's shared and how the vision's cast? So, I would just encourage as you're thinking about that, just one of the tips to be thinking about.

As you're recruiting, probably one more thought I'd share on that. Think about the reach of your team. Often when we're recruiting, we're kind of doing this ... We start to go about it ourselves, right? We're like, "Oh, okay who can I think of?" You usually end up with a list of 10, 20, maybe 30 people that you know, and you reach out to them, but then you can't get very far past that.

But if you think about your current kid's ministry team, maybe ask them, "Hey, who do you think we could reach out to about serving in kid's ministry?" Or maybe even better than that, maybe they could make the ask for you to serve in kid's ministry. I've found that to be the most effective recruiting tool I've ever used. When people on my kid's ministry teams have gone out and said, "Hey, I really love doing this. I think you'd be a good fit to do this, too."

So, those are just a few thoughts, as far as just tips. But as far as your strategies, one of the questions that comes up a lot is, "Okay, how do I get people to join?" Once I've practiced the ask, and casting vision, and things like that, how do I get them to join? A few thoughts on that just real briefly.

One is, sometimes you can figure out what a good first experience is. I've had a lot of kid's ministry leaders or volunteers that started in kid's ministry just helping out with the VBS or something like that. Something really small, and they really enjoyed it, and they said, "Oh, I want to keep doing this." And from there, they continued to serve. So, be thinking about that, those first experiences.

But then also when you're asking people, give them a picture of what they're signing up for. So, maybe you're going to say, "Oh, we're going to ask for you to serve for a year, and maybe you can re-up after that." Or you might decide "Hey, let's do nine months, fall and spring, and three months off in the summer." Kind of gives people a break if they want to take summer off and then come back in. So, there are just a few thoughts there as we think about recruiting and how we can do that well.

After we've recruited volunteers, how do we go about developing them?

As we talk about developing our volunteers, I have three thoughts on that. We think about Initial Training, Ongoing Coaching, and Deeper Training. Those are the three areas to talk about a little bit. First, the Initial Training. Just thinking about having them observe our ministry and leaders and kids. Anything that we can do in that initial training with our new volunteers where they can observe and see things going on. It helps give them a picture of how they can be interacting with kids and with other leaders, things like that.

A model that I like to share is a four-step model. First is, "I do. You watch." So they're watching you do it. The second step is, "I do. You help." We're transitioning away from a new person watching, and now they're beginning to help and get some experience. And then the next step of that, the third one is, "You do. I help." You're transferring some of that ownership, but you're still kind of involved. And then the fourth one is, "You do. I watch." At that point you're going. "You got it!" and I'm just checking to make sure… "Hey, are we doing well?" I've found that model works very well with new volunteers.

The second thought as we're developing our volunteers is Ongoing Coaching. I think the best thing that we can do for our volunteers is to be coaching them along the way. Giving feedback as we're going. So, think about "How do we even share feedback?".

One of my favorite methods I like to share is the Oreo Method. So, when you're sharing feedback, you're evaluating someone, think about sharing something positive, right? The outside of that Oreo. Share something positive. What are they doing well? And then when you get to that middle part. That's kind of the good spot for that constructive feedback. "Hey, I think here's an area of improvement." That's where you're able to share that with them. And then always ending the other side of that Oreo on the positive note.

I've heard it called the sandwich method, too, but everyone loves Oreos, so that's always good, too! You know what I mean?

I encourage you as you're providing that ongoing coaching, just focus on one or two areas of feedback at a time as far as growth. Because for most of us, really, we can only grow in a few areas at once. Choose one area, or maybe if you've got a high-capacity leader or a volunteer, maybe you could do two.

And then the third area is Deeper Training. Doing in-depth sessions where you can go through training. So, explore what that looks like for your context. What does that look like for ours? We do a once-a-year training where we do a deep dive. Multiple hours of training. Really investing in our volunteers in that way. I know there are a lot of resources out now where you can do video trainings, and send video links out. I think those are helpful, too. Those are some different ways you can do kind of that deeper dive training.

We've looked at recruiting and developing our volunteers. A big problem is retaining our volunteers! How do we do that?

As we think about retaining our volunteers, a few quick thoughts on that. One is thinking about encouragement. I think it's so key to provide that encouragement to our volunteers. For some of us, it comes naturally. For some of us, we don't practice it as much. I really do think that all of our leaders in kid's ministry need to be doing that on a regular basis, week in, week out. Looking for the little things and ways we can continue to encourage our volunteers, because that really helps.

When they're doing something well, encourage them. When someone encourages you, I mean, that's really uplifting, and it really does encourage you to continue doing what you're doing. You might think, "Hey, they noticed I did a really good job at this. I'm going to keep doing that and try to do my best in that area." Any time we can encourage, I think it's always helpful.

Good communication's another one. That always helps in teams. It's kind of like marriage. You've got a lot of issues that may come up if you don't have good communication, right? So, it's the same way with your teams, your volunteer teams. Communication is key. Good communication goes a long way to retaining a volunteer. That's a big deal!

Also, be thinking about community. When people come to serve, they're not only spending that time with the kids and investing in them, but they're also spending time with those other volunteers. So, create a community.

Maybe there's a way that you can create that. Maybe when they come to serve, is there a few minutes where they're able to connect with some of the other volunteers? Or, maybe we're talking about an occasional, "Hey, we're going to do a get together. We're going to have fun." And all the volunteers get together, and we're going to spend time together. It just helps create that community, because people love to be a part of a community! It's often one of the reasons why they've signed up. Often it's to invest in the kids, but it's also to be a part of that community as well.

So, be thinking about how you can cultivate that community as the kid's ministry leader. And think about how you're developing people, because people do love to grow. Some will grow faster than others, and that's okay. Just thinking about how you can provide those opportunities for growth and developing them.

And lastly, I'd say just appreciation. You're spending time encouraging them. Also just say "Thank you." "I really appreciate the hard work you're putting in." "I appreciate how you took the time to sit with Johnny and answer some of his questions." Or "I love how kind you were talking to Suzy when she wanted to go on and on about her cat, Fluffy. You were so kind in just talking to her, and helping her learn the lesson today."

And look for ways to appreciate them. Both verbally and then maybe occasionally a very small gift. No one's looking for $100 gift cards from you for serving in kid's ministry. But maybe just some little small gift just to encourage them and appreciate them.

This was great. Thank you so much Steven. I really appreciate you taking the time to help us recruit, develop, and retain our volunteers.

Hey, thank you, Keith.

Steven Knight

Steven is the founder of KidMinTools.com and the Family Life Pastor at Fellowship Bible Church in Waco, TX. He is the author of Recruit: How to Find Volunteers for Ministry and is a contributing author for several kidmin books. He enjoys speaking at ministry conferences and church special events. Steven has almost 15 years of ministry experience, earned a ThM from Dallas Theological Seminary, and lives in Waco with his wife Katie and two sons.

How do I effectively communicate with parents?

I'm here today with Amber Lappin. Thank you so much for joining me today.

Happy to be here.

Before we dive into this topic of communicating with parents, give us a little bit of your journey in children's ministry and what context you serve in now.

Okay, I started as a preschool teacher, and I wound up serving in my church, which was a mobile church. We met in a school gym and had to move in and out of that a bunch. Eventually, we grew to a large enough size that we really needed somebody to do training and recruiting and caring for the volunteers, and that's when I came on staff, at about nine years into that. I was able to use the training I had in early education to be able to train and equip our 350 volunteers. So, I went from a tiny little tiny church to a medium-sized church to a giant church, and then I really got to start finding out that my calling was not necessarily in the classroom, although I still get to play in a classroom, but really in caring for adults - the people who care for children. That led me eventually working as a director, as a trainer, starting my own training around the world, and then finally, I was able to go back to school, get my bachelor's and my master's and start teaching at the local community college. That's actually my ministry right now. Caring for all these young adults who are just starting to care for children and help them to see how beautifully complex children learn and grow and how we can be a source of support and love for kids.

So I get to do that. I also have a couple other jobs. I work for another community college as a foster parent care educator. I also get to write, so I do a lot of different writing. And I just get to support parents and teachers and children's ministers all over the world. I just love it! This is exactly what I was meant to do, and I enjoy every minute of it.

That's great. This topic of communication that we're going to focus on today – communication is such a huge thing, and everybody wants to improve it. We're going to look at once slice of that "communication pie" that is so important to people who work in children's ministry, and that is improving our communication with parents. I know you've got some really practical things on how we can improve that, even from what we do with our tone and our body, so I'd love for you to unpack a bit of how do we improve communication with parents?

I think that communicating with parents is one of those things that's fairly universal. It seems like it should be so easy, but it can be such a fear for some people. Or a bad experience can happen, causing a person to avoid communicating with parents. Or some people are really great with kids, and adults are not their thing. What we found is that if we build solid relationships with parents first, communication is going to go so much better, especially if we have to ever bring up anything negative. To begin, I suggest that churches make sure that the person that is at the door greeting children when they come into the church should be somebody who is happy to be there. If you're the person who just has to have an extra hour after they get to church to be friendly, the door of the children's ministry classroom is not a place for you. .

We want somebody who is excited to be there and who can greet every single child, then parent in a welcoming way. So like I purposefully said, first, we greet the children. Then, we greet the parents. That shows parents that we have an eye out for their children. I think sometimes, people forget how weird it is to drop off children with strangers because we're in children's ministry for a long time. We might even roll our eyes at parents who are hesitant to do it. But we don't realize how hard it is for parents. There's a lot of evidence that they should be nervous about leaving their children with people they don't know. So who need to respect that and make every effort to make them feel secure as they're leaving their children. Not only is our communication going to be better with them, but our experience with the children is going to be better as well.

I recommend always welcoming children as warmly as possible. Even if a baby is sleeping, and they're handing them to you in a car seat, and they're just sacked out, you still whisper hello and then say, "Hi, I'm so glad you brought him. Come on in." But you're always greeting the parents positively. Though the warm welcoming part may be fairly well known, the part I think where we forget is how important it is at pickup time for us to communicate with parents. When parents begin to arrive again, you need to have somebody exciting at that door to greet the parents as they come in, and then we should have a second person in the classroom doing an activity with the children, where all the children are actually facing away from the door, so they're not watching all their parents come and feeling like they're being left behind. Then they start crying because they haven't seen their parent. They are shaping the parents' image of what's been happening the whole time they were gone is that their child has been crying when they were probably fine.

So, if you can face the children away from the door and have somebody come up and help the children individually come toward the door when their parent comes, then that's going to have a better, smoother transition, and then if that person can just say one positive thing – mention something that happened. "Oh my gosh, your child is so good at memorizing the books of the Bible." Or "Man, your child is very creative! I was so amazed at how good they are at building things out of blocks." I have had to get desperate sometimes. I'm like "Wow, your child has great shoes." Everyone can come up with something positive you can say about their child, so that way, they know that you notice their child, that you know who they are, that that child is special to you. If you can do all of that for a parent, then they're going to feel like you love their child.

When you're a stranger, parents don't have a way to know their children will be safe until you prove it. It's your job to prove that you care about their child, that you want them to do well, and that you want them to be happy and cared for just the same way that they do. If you can do that, then when it's time to talk to them about anything else, then you already have that relationship, that friendship.

That's great. That really tees up the second question, which is, "When is it okay to talk to parents about negative behavior, and how do you go about having that conversation?" Because it's not always, "Hey, everything went great, and I love everything from your shoes to your creativity to your memorization techniques. Sometimes things don't go well.

You're right.

What do you do there?

I think the first thing that we have to bear in mind is that parents who have children who behave badly generally know this. You're not telling them something brand new, like you're the first person to give them this information. They probably already know. They are probably already afraid of what you're going to say. That doesn't mean that all children are always naughty all the time or that the naughty children are only ever naughty, but I mean the children who are just rascals on a regular basis, this is not new to the parents. They already have to hear it from the teachers at school. They already have to hear it at Boy Scouts. They already have to hear it at powderpuff, soccer or karate. They know this already.

So, we don't have to feel like we're in charge of informing a child or a parent that their child is a problem. Instead, first, we have to really look at our own motives for why we want to talk to the parents about the negative behavior. Is there something a parent can even do? Sometimes, I think that we might say to parents, "Oh, they didn't sit very still today." But the parent was in church! How are they supposed to keep their child sitting still from way from their seat in the sanctuary? You couldn't do it, and you were sitting right there! And you're an expert.

When parents get information about their children's negative behavior, it should be paired with something that they could actually do. When I'm thinking about when to tell a parent something negative, the first thing I need to consider is, do they need to know about it at all? I don't mean hiding information or keeping secrets. But I just mean, if you got in trouble already at church, do you have to be in trouble at home about it too? Or could it just be over? Could we just give fresh mercies and could we just say "Don't do that again" and it's over? Sometimes, we can't. Sometimes we have to notify parents, of course. Certainly!

One time, I was in a classroom with a child who had told all of the children that he was going to cut them with the knife in his pocket – which was actually there! That's not something I can wait on. That's not tattling. That's an emergency! The reason I use that example is because I think it should be about that extreme if you're going to talk to families about something negative the first couple times they come.

Instead, children should have at least three weeks of coming to church and trying to figure out how it works before we're tattling to their parents when they show up at the door. Sometimes, people will ask. What if the parents ask? Because remember, I told you that parents of naughty children are ready for this. They ask, "Did they hit anybody? Did they bite? Did they kick? How did they behave?" If a parent is asking, they probably are waiting for the worst.

In this instance, a good answer could be, "We're just getting settled in. It's our first week…It's only the second week…It's only the third week." The parent could wonder, "Oh, does that mean they were terrible?" "Well, no. It means that we're getting settled in, and I promise I will tell you if it becomes a problem or if there's anything."

That's good.

That gives the parents just a little bit of freedom to relax. I can't imagine going to church service being so nervous about whether or not my child was going to get kicked out of church on my first or second week. I'm already trying to figure out when you're supposed to stand up and sit down and when do we have to pray and how do we … what's the tune of this song? You're already figuring all that out. You're also worried that as soon as you go pick up your child, you're going to have to hear an earful about how terrible they are. Why would you go back? You can stay home in bed, and you don't have to hear it. So I try to give it three weeks. Just three weeks of trying to get settled in and try things. Because we also know about children that they behave weird when they're not familiar with situations. They have to test people. They have to test places. Ask any substitute teacher. They know. As soon as there's an unfamiliar adult in the room, then the rules have to be tested all over again.

So, allow three weeks for adjustment. And then after that, if you're like "Wow, this behavior is just not stopping," then of course you want to talk to the parents. You just need to figure out ahead of time, "What could I do? What could the parent do to help me? What am I asking of this parent?" One time, we had a child who had special needs in one of our classrooms. Every time the door would open, she would just run out, and she was the fastest child I've seen. We would just be running after her, trying to catch her before she'd get out the door. After about three weeks of trying everything we could think of doing, putting a bell on the door, attempting everything we could think of, we finally asked, "What do you do?" Hoping she must know a trick. And she says, "Oh my goodness, I'm so sorry. I should have told you. She thinks that if she's not wearing shoes, then she can't go outside. So if you just take off her shoes, she'll be fine."

Man. Of course, it's usually not that easy. That's why that story stands out. But sometimes, the purpose of telling a parent, talking to a parent about behavior is because you're literally stumped. You don't know what to do, and you would like some tips. You have to be ready, though, because sometimes the tips are not going to be something you're willing to do. I've had parents say, "No, we just spank them." Okay, can't do that. Or "We just put Tabasco on his tongue." All right. That's not going to work in class. Sometimes, you're not going to get help. But that might also let them open a door to say, "I don't know what to do. Tell me." And then that's a good way to build that relationship.

But I think that if you're thinking through, "What could the parent possibly do about this situation? What do I want them to do?" Maybe you want them to empty their pockets before checking them into class. Or maybe you want them to leave their toy behind because bringing the toy is a problem. Or maybe you would like the parents to bring them a little earlier so that they have some time to get settled. Or take them to a different age classroom because they're walking now and knocking down all the children and they need to be in an older classroom. If you have something that they can do, then absolutely you should have that conversation. But if it can just be a matter of letting it go and letting it just be a grace moment, then I would say every time you can do that, you should. Just give that child a break from being in trouble and enjoy the look on their face when their parents say, "How did it go?" And you say, "Well, we learned about Noah's Ark today!" It was a great day. And watch the child's face, and they're thinking, "Wow, I'm not going to be grounded on my way home from church. Finally!" I think that's a good way to go.

Thank you so much. This has been great! As many conversations as I've had about communication and doing ministry, I'm just hearing some of these practical phrases to say, and how to position kids in the room to make some of that easier. And how to tee up conversations. I think that's some of what's standing out to me right now is even thinking about how much communication is improved by the preparatory conversations. About greeting people and building that relationship ahead of time and setting that expectation of "Hey, this is a place that we actually want your kid."

I really, really appreciate you taking the time. I feel like I want to have a conversation with you about kids at church and a conversation with you about my own kids! [Laughs] Anyhow, thank you so much for taking the time, Amber. I really appreciate it.

My pleasure.

Amber Lappin

Amber Lappin first met Jesus in a children's ministry classroom when she was just a little girl. It is her life's passion to equip people who work with children so they can see kids through God's eyes. Now, she trains teachers, parents, volunteers, and leaders at churches, parenting groups, and schools. She also works as a professor at her local college in the early childhood education department. Amber holds a BS in Human Development and a M.Ed. in Early Childhood Education. Currently, she lives in Southern California with her husband and enjoys spending time with her three grownup kids – twin daughters who are college students and a son who works with the fire department.

DAN LOVAGLIA

How do I foster "relational" family ministry?

I'm here today with Dan Lovaglia. Thanks so much for joining me, Dan.

You bet, Keith. Thanks.

Give us a rundown of your ministry journey, what different places you've served, and what context you're in now.

Wow! Ok. I became a Christian as a kid, so children's ministry literally changed my life. I'd say that Christ-centered children's ministry was what transformed me. Grew up in the church – after quite an adventure of a home life. Was called into ministry in high school, like a lot of guys my age, and during the years when a lot of people were mentoring me and building into me.

Ended up going to Moody Bible Institute for youth ministry. Became a youth pastor right out of that. Served in a small little church, ran youth ministry, junior high, high school, college. Kind of did the whole burnout thing, and so I quit. Went back to get a master's in evangelism and spiritual formation, and that was a soul-enriching time.

I ended up at a huge church. So, I've been in small churches, medium-sized churches, and mega churches. Worked in children's ministry at a mega church in the Chicagoland area. Was also the teaching and content director for adult discipleship and wrote tons of curriculum and classes and so on, and then ended up moving on from there and was in the nonprofit ministry world with a global children's/youth ministry program called Awana for five years.

From there, I have moved on and I'm now a nationwide staffing and coaching consultant with Slingshot Group. We're a group of 55+ associates across the country, and we get to serve in all different kinds of churches, partnering with individuals, candidates, organizations, walking with them as they find remarkable team players in their churches/ministries.

That really tees up my next question. Since you've seen so many different sizes and types of churches in all different stages of your own ministry journey, talk to me about the question that every church asks and the conversation, when it comes to children's ministry, that every church has. What is that question and what is that conversation?

Oh, every church. Every church. It's the same question that you ask at Thanksgiving— "What do we do with the kids?" Every church is wondering when we gather together, do the kids get to sit with us as the adults? Or, do the kids sit at the kid's table? Essentially, do the kids participate with us or is this an adult-only, faith formation experience?

Whatever is happening, it's very much like any family holiday. "What do we do with the kids?" drives decisions. They [church leaders] are trying to figure out, do we educate them? Do we play with them? Do we teach them how to sing worship songs at their own age level and so on? What is our view of disciple-making? These are the questions that every church is wrestling with, and everyone has different answers and rationales for why they do one thing over another.

There's a phrase that, as you've seen this conversation happen over and over again, you keep coming back to, which is "relational children's ministry." In fact, you ended up writing a book with that title. I want to spend most of our time looking at these "invitations" – as you call them – to how to do it. But first take a minute and just define what you mean by "relational children's ministry."

As I've talked with leaders, both in training and coaching settings and also informally, just having coffee with lots of people, individual disciples, leaders, they all recognize that they should be a deeply devoted follower of Christ first, then that gets poured into the lives of others.

What they're describing is relational ministry! The relational disciple-making that happens in the church. As I've thought about children's ministry, and done research on this, it's the same thing. What holds people? What keeps people rooted in the family of faith? It always comes down to relationship—relationship with God, relationship with other people.

If you take a look at something like [the book] You Lost Me by David Kinnaman, that research points to a whole bunch of issues as to why people walk away from God or walk away from the family of faith. And it all comes down to a relational problem. It's a disciple-making problem. It's not simply about a broken system or a program.

At the beginning of it all, relational children's ministry is recognizing that every one of us is a kid influencer. Kids influence peers. Adults influence kids. Kids influence adults. We're all children in the family of God.

Proverbs 22:6 is real clear. "Train up a child in the way that he or she will go and when they're old, they won't turn from it."

There are two parts to that. One is, they're going to walk with God in the way that He made them, and they're not going to turn from that. We also have a responsibility to walk with them, train them up, and hopefully we do that second part in the right way. Relational disciple-making has to be at the core of the church. I believe it starts with children, because that's how that [the body of Christ] gets multiplied— age by age by age, generation to generation.

Okay. Moving from what it is to how we actually do it, you center that conversation around five invitations. Let's take a look at each one of those. What are they?

Sure. There are five invitations. As you look at Jesus' disciple-making model, he always paid attention to people. His starting point was to look people in the eye, get to know who they were, exactly how they worked, and he never told them. He invited: "Come follow me."

INVITATION #1: DRAW KIDS INTO AN UNSCRIPTED ADVENTURE WITH GOD

"Come, follow me," Jesus said, "and I will send you out to fish for people." Mark 1:17

The first invitation is very simple. Draw kids into an unscripted adventure. Draw kids into an unscripted adventure with God. What we like to do with kids is we like to tell them every step of the way so that they don't put a fork in a light socket, or so that they don't get in a fight with somebody.

What is it really? It's about us fearfully wanting to manage this mess that could happen instead of faithfully allowing the adventure of discipleship to happen. The best adventures happen when we let it be unscripted, and that's how Jesus was. He just said, "Follow me. Drop everything. Let's go."

I think that there's a principle here for children's ministry, which is: Fear follows the script. You get a curriculum. You put it in front of you, right? This is the curriculum [holds up paper]: Follow this. Read it from the top to the bottom, and so you have leaders that look at it and they go, [Looking down at paper reading] "Uh...Hello...Keith."

But let's say you were their leader for 10 years and you're still following the script!

You'd start with a question...use their name...make eye contact. Not... say this...say this...do this...answer this...do the next activity...and move on.

That's not how we walk with God! And so, how do we model that unscripted adventure that all of us want to be on?

Okay. Draw kids into an unscripted adventure with God. Invitation one. What is invitation two?

If you go back to Jesus' words, same as with the first one, "Follow me." When you go to the second one, it's simply, "Wrestle with messy faith together. Wrestle with messy faith together."

INVITATION #2: WRESTLE WITH MESSY FAITH TOGETHER

"Come to me, all you who are weary and burdened, and I will give you rest." Matthew 11:28

A lot of us like to tell our faith story about: 1. How I came to know Jesus, and 2. My life has been this way ever since. We don't want to give kids the details of where that hasn't been exactly "up and to the right." All of us would agree that rather than a straight line starting here [points to bottom of screen], we trust and follow Christ and then it just goes up [pointing to top of screen] and now we're loving God and loving people...then, one fine day I'll fly away, here we go!

That's not how it happens! It looks more like this, right? [Makes squiggly, up-and-down line with index finger.] It's this crazy, unscripted adventure full of twists and turns. How do we as adults or kid influencers of younger ages work with children, walk alongside them, and agree that this is an adventure and it's unscripted and it's messy? How do we allow for the messiness of faith to be part of the story?

Something that's not only true for me, though it comes out of my story, is that there was divorce and there was alcohol and drug abuse and all kinds of weird stuff going on in my home. And we had a family that welcomed us in, my mom and me. She[my mother] was a single mom, with an atheist, feminist background. Yet, there was someone in our life who welcomed us in fully. Right in the middle of the mess they just modeled what was true in Scripture, what was true in the church community, and we became adopted into this spiritual family. Well, that was huge! We had a place to process the mess.

In children's ministry, what I've found is if we can find ways to help kids come away with three different virtues, three different virtues that we model and we exhibit with them and also in our own lives, that can change everything.

The first one is simply presence. Consistently being present and communicating to kids, "I'm here." If you have a round robin rotation system where you only have people serving every six weeks, it's terrible. They [children] can't identify with that person because they never know who their leader's going to be. Every other week would be fine. You have Keith and me. We lead a guy's small group. They know if Keith's not there, I'm there. They can remember that, but imagine in school having a different teacher every day all the time! Never knowing who they are. They just come off a list and they're a substitute. So... presence. "I'm here."

The second one is humility. How often do you hear in children's ministry adults saying, "I don't know"? We always have an answer. We've got to come up with some spiritual answer, something out of Scripture, something out of our own life. Why can't, when some kid asks us, "How in the world was Jesus human and divine?," why do we have to come up with an illustration? Why can't we just say, "I don't know. Here's what scripture says. Let's explore it together"?

That leads to the next principle, so there's presence, humility, and then empathy. Not just, "I'm here," and not just, "I don't know," but then to also say, "We're in this together." When the kid says, "Hey, I'm going through my parents' divorce," or, "I don't understand what's going on with the economy. We might have to sell our house," that we can be right there with them. We know what that [tough situation] is like.

One of the best ways for this kind of stuff to happen is to give a 3-by-5 card to every kid. Have them write down a prayer request, something they're struggling with in their home, and then put them up on the wall. You and your leaders could stand there and look at that wall. Pray over it. Kids go home, and then, you could stand there [as leaders] and look at that wall at the end of your hour and know what's going on in their hearts. It's messy. It's very, very messy. Deal with that first instead of following that script.

Good. All right, so invitation three. Tell us about that.

Invitation three is: build unconventional bridges [between church and home]. I love to be unconventional. We must build unconventional community with families.

INVITATION #3: BUILD UNCONVENTIONAL COMMUNITY WITH FAMILIES

"My command is this: Love each other as I have loved you." John 15:12

We're all familiar with conventional bridges [between church and home]. Conventional bridges are these. You walk in [to a church's children's ministry] and immediately there's a sign that says, "You should sign up to serve. We have a 90-minute experience. You dropped your kid off. You owe us 90 minutes. We need you to serve."

Well, that doesn't make sense. You don't want everybody who comes to your ministry to serve. There are going to be people who are in need of care and shelter and compassion first. You do not want my atheist mom serving as a small group leader. Don't put up a big sign that says, "Everyone should serve," right?

Now, something that's true in these kinds of relationships is that we're talking about loving each other wherever we're at. The first bridge when you're thinking about building unconventional communities. That's the first bridge, "The Care Bridge." You're basically trying to help that group of people who just need space to come in, drop their kid off, and it's okay. Give them a $5 Starbucks card, and tell them to go away. Go have a date night. Go shopping. Go whatever. Don't try and sell them on a co-op.

"The Coaching Bridge" comes next. You've got some other people that need to be coached and they need some equipping, some timely tools and resources. Coach them. Work with them. Walk with them. But don't just tell them how to be the "best parent," because it just hurts their feelings. They know they're not the best parent! It's okay to have a class called Parenting is Hard and I'm No Good at It. You all commiserate and go home, but to have a class on the 42 Ways You Should Be A Better Parent? People come and they never come back to your church.

Then there's challenge, a third bridge, and that's "The Challenge Bridge." You have to be able to challenge people. Some people need to be told to step it up. Model something for other families. Model something for other leaders. We want to build a bridge with that family that isn't going to walk with Christ, has no idea what the church is, doesn't understand the gospel at all. We've got to figure out how do we help them. How do we help them? We need some role models, and mentors, to step it up.

We also need some families to chill out. That's the other option. Just look at some parents and they will tell you, "I'm not doing it well enough." They're serving in every ministry. They come to every service. They do every activity they're ever told, on and on. And they always tell themselves they fall short. Sometimes you just need to tell them to chill out—"You've got this. You've got this!" You start communicating those messages—step it up and chill out. It's actually much more invitational. It's an unconventional way of building a bridge.

What's the simplest way? The simplest way for this unconventional community to happen? Do ministry in the park and invite families with kids. Just say, "We're going to meet at this park in this afternoon every Tuesday. See you there."

Who's in charge of security? All the parents. Who's in charge of food? Whoever brings it. Who's in charge of the curriculum? The kids. They make the up the games together and you just hang out. Then, when you [the pastor/director/leader] has got to go home, you're like, "It's time for me to go home. You guys all keep having fun." You won't be able to keep them apart from each other and they will feel loved and served and welcome.

That's great. I love those three bridges. That's a perfect analogy. Invitation four, you say, is to model Christ's life-transforming mission. Tell us more about that invitation.

Yes. Matthew 28. We're all familiar with the great commission and children's ministry has tipped over into the Not-So-Great Commission. "Go and go and go, make programs, administrate all things, and don't lose any children or families."—that's not the Great Commission! The Great Commission is actually "Go and make disciples of all nations, baptizing them in the name of the Father and of the Son and of the Holy Spirit, and teaching them to obey everything I have commanded you. And lo, I am with you always, to the very end of the age."

INVITATION #4: MODEL CHRIST'S LIFE-TRANSFORMING MISSION

Then Jesus came to them and said, "All authority in heaven and on earth has been given to me. Therefore go and make disciples of all nations, baptizing them in the name of the Father and of the Son and of the Holy Spirit, and teaching them to obey everything I have commanded you. And surely I am with you always, to the very end of the age." Matthew 28:18-20

The verse before that is all about the Holy Spirit and the power and the authority that's being passed upon us. Most kids have no idea that we, as leaders, have a life outside of the lanyard we wear. We sit there with our curriculum and our lanyard and they see us there. They have no idea that we have a family, that we have a job, that we have to wrestle with all the messy faith and the unscripted adventure outside of the environment that we're in. For you...and for me...we need to have kids be able to see a window into a full transformation. Like a butterfly is being transformed completely.

In my life, I had all kinds of mentors and leaders and people who demonstrated a life outside of the program, outside of the church building, and outside in the real world. It was formative and changed me because I actually saw: 1. They believed I could be a disciple-maker and I could be a kid influencer, but also 2. They also wanted me to be part of their life outside, so I could see the whole picture, the whole transformation.

I talked with a ministry recently and they said, "We're just going to videotape people like Keith or other leaders in our ministry. They're going to go out and videotape their day. So, they're maybe a volunteer in their ministry. We're going to videotape them at work, and at home, and having dinner, and whatever. Then we're going to show that to our kids and highlight the Volunteer of the Month or Volunteer of the Week. That way they can see that this person has a real life as a real follower of Christ outside of this 1-hour experience together."

That's great. We've got one more invitation: To equip children for dynamic discipleship. I love that phrase – dynamic discipleship. Tell us more.

Yes. I think of the metaphor of having headphones. When you have headphones, you're able to listen and to hear and then you have a choice, obey or don't obey, right? I'm going to do this, not do this, let it influence me, not influence me. Jesus was pretty clear. He's like, "I want you to listen to my voice. My sheep, I know them. They know me. They listen to my voice. They follow me."

INVITATION #5: EQUIP CHILDREN FOR DYNAMIC DISCIPLESHIP

"My sheep listen to my voice; I know them, and they follow me." John 10:27

That's what we want. We want dynamic discipleship so that kids are prepared to make decisions, prepared to walk with Christ day-by-day, moment-by-moment, listening—turn left, turn right, do this, don't do that, ask questions, be curious, and so on. How do we equip them in the ways that needs to happen?

Another metaphor to consider. Kids come in for the church service and we say, "What do we do with them?" We put them over here in this wing of the church or in the basement. [Laughs] Always the basement, of course! We put them over there, and then we have them basically run around a track. Just run around the track. And we'll do a curriculum and we'll do some games and we'll do some small group and it's fine. But they never learn to run cross country!

As a [dynamic] disciple-maker, we have a responsibility to equip them so they can go out into the world and run cross country with Christ in community. That's our goal, to run cross country together, not to just run in a circle and then say, "Game over, put your uniform away and go home."

Okay. Well, I think the overwhelming thought as I hear you unpack these invitations is thinking of all the churches I've been in, and how these invitations would be fleshed out differently in different contexts. There's a need to sit down with your volunteers, to sit down with your parents, to sit down with the church staff and to have discussions about these invitations. How does this play out in our context? Or even in this season? Because it may be that a year from now, it's different. It almost seems like these five invitations would be a fantastic guide for an annual conversation.

Absolutely.

Thank you so much for taking the time to unpack these invitations with us and for your passion and heart for children's ministers and the kids that they serve. Thank you.

Thanks so much. I appreciate it.

Dan Lovaglia

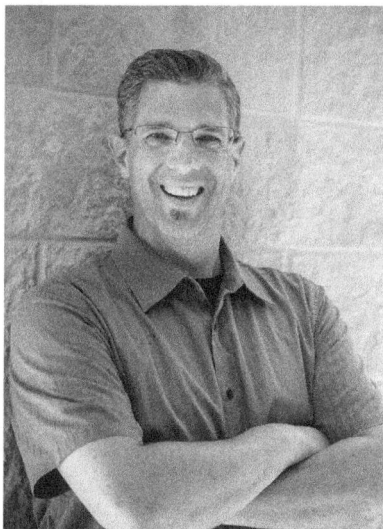

Dan Lovaglia is the author of Relational Children's Ministry: Turning Kid-Influencers into Lifelong Disciple Makers and a staffing/coaching associate at Slingshot Group for children's & family ministries. He equips church leaders nationwide through writing, speaking, consulting, and training. Connect with Dan on Twitter and Facebook @DanLovaglia

STANLEY MEARSE

How do I successfully minister to tweens?

I am here with Stanley Mearse. Thank you so much for coming and joining me.

Oh, it's an honor. I'm glad to be here.

Before we dive in – to tee this up – to what it means to S.P.O.I.L. a tween tell us a little bit about your ministry journey and what context you serve in right now.

Ministry for me started out at a young age as a volunteer summer missionary through college. I got to work with children that way. Then I got my undergraduate in Elementary Education. I really enjoyed teaching children new things and watching that lightbulb go off. Then I thought, "If you could teach a child the gospel, then you can teach anybody the gospel!" I went onto seminary, planning to be a head pastor, but when I was there it just didn't fit. It wasn't right.

When I was serving in my first church outside of seminary I really felt called to Children's Ministry. I said, "Can you make a living at this? Is it even possible?" [Laughs] God opened doors, and I've been at several churches from average attendance of 1,300 a week all the way down to 400 a week of average attendance and in between. Right now I'm at Mountain View Baptist Church in Hickory, North Carolina. We have an average attendance of about 650 a Sunday. It's growing by leaps and bounds, and God's moving. I'm just glad to be a part and serve with Him.

How many kids do you have coming through...let's say preschool through fifth grade?

On average from preschool to 6th grade, we run around 150 per Sunday.

Right. Specifically today...Well, I feel like I'd want to have ten more conversations with you about the specific areas that you are passionate about. But today, I want to hone in on tweens. So before we dive into the what, the why, and the how, what is your definition of a tween? Who are they?

A tween is a fifth and sixth grader. They're at the point where they think they're ready to go to the youth group because they feel like children's ministry is a little too childish for them, but they're not really emotionally or spiritually ready for the youth group yet. So they're begging their parents not to go to church. They want to drop out. It's usually the lower number you have inside the children's ministry area. Then trying to go, "What do we do with them? They're causing problems. Trying to push back on authority."

Right. Fifth and sixth graders. For different people reading this, sixth grade is already part of that youth group. At my church, sixth grade is a part of that middle school youth group. But I grew up where it was seventh grade that youth group started, so the fifth, sixth grade, I completely know... [Laughs] Because that was definitely where I was in my church context 100 years ago when I was a tween!

It also depends on the school district in that area. They're the ones who usually define that for the churches.

Yeah, definitely. We'll get into the how in just a second. We talked about the "what." Now, the "why." This idea, can a tween really handle the responsibility of serving in the church? What do you feel like the Bible says about that? I know you're passionate about that.

Oh yes. Scripture's the way to go. That's where you start everything. It's God's words, living and breathing. There are several different scriptures to go to, like Mark 10:14 or Proverbs 22:6. But the one that you really need to hit it home with is the Great Commission. It's Matthew 28:19-20. Because when a child accepts Jesus as their Lord and Savior, and they have the Holy Spirit inside of them, the Bible doesn't put an age limit on who is supposed to go and make disciples.

He says we're all supposed to go and make disciples of all nations. Jesus didn't stop the children from coming to him. He said, "Let the children come to me." The Kingdom of Heaven belongs to them, and they need to be living and leading and serving just like the rest of us.

Amen. For the rest of our conversation, I want to hone in on "how." I know you've trained your leaders and volunteers, and how to think specifically about tween ministry using an acronym that at first blush causes people in today's day and age to cringe. Because you believe we should "spoil tweens."

Yes. I like the play on words there.

So before people stop reading, ha ha, let's dive in. What is the "S" in spoil?

The "S" in S.P.O.I.L. is "Scripture." Like I said, you need to start with the Word of God. Before you do any ministry, before you reach out to anybody, you need to know what the Bible says. What God says to you. That's what we're supposed to be getting across, is be obedient to God and serving Him by His Word. So that's the reason we go to the Scripture first on anything. That's the S in S.P.O.I.L.. What does the Word of God have to say?

Then what's the "P?"

The P is…What's the "Purpose?" Why are we doing this? Why would you want to invest in this? Well, it's for discipleship. That's the first part, because we're called as adults to go make disciples as well. We need to be investing in the people we come in contact with the most, and that's the children. It's a great way to start that discipleship process with them. It helps with the leadership. If they're preforming in children's worship, it helps with stage presence, so they're not scared of being in front of people or their peers. It fosters relationship building, obedience, and fosters a servant's heart. And it lets your talents blossom and grow as well. So if they like singing, they're not afraid of the crowds. They can hone in on those talents. Maybe they're better at puppets or drama.

Then also, people are the body of Christ. That is kind of the purpose and vision behind it in a nutshell.

Along that line...what triggered in my mind right there is...When you're sharing purpose, do find that it's easier, or harder, that there are different ways that you approach discussing purpose when you're talking to the leaders about spoiling the tweens? Or when you're talking to the tweens themselves? Whose more accepting of hearing and receiving this idea of purpose of their ministry?

It's their parent's! Their parent's see that they actually have a purpose for being there. They're tweens that aren't involved in church are being invested in. It shows that you care about them and thought about them. The parents get excited! The kids get excited because they ...well, the first year it's a little bit hard, because you've got to convince the first ones to step on stage. But then the next fourth grader is going, "I want to do that! If they can do it, I can do it!" And they can't wait.

Then, your leaders are going, "There's something here. There's an excitement that hasn't been there. We're seeing God move." Then before long they're going, "We need this to happen!" So, then there's total buy-in. But the first people to really catch on and excited are the parents.

That's great. That's great. Yeah, you get parents onboard, that's a huge, huge win! That's a big struggle for many family ministry folks, for sure.

Yes, sir.

So, we've got the S, we've got the P, so what's the "O" in S.P.O.I.L.?

The "O" in S.P.O.I.L. is "Observe." You need to know who you're working with. You need to know the tween, where they're at. You need to know what they're into. First of all, we mainly have it for our worship team. We do stuff outside of worship as well. Do they like puppets? Do they like singing? Do they like running computers and tech? Do they like helping with game time? Who are they? So you've got to observe them.

Then you've got to identify their gifts and talents and where their heart is. You need to see what available roles you have. Then you need to determine what motivates and encourages the tween. That's spending time with them, and knowing their background, and getting to know their families, what family dynamic they come from. So, how to interact, who they are, and observe them personally one-on-one.

Let's unpack that a little bit. When you're observing, how much of the observing is truly how we traditionally think about that word? Where you're just spending time watching that kid do something, or taking note...and how do you capture that? I mean you've got a big ministry of kids. Of your 100 and something kids, how many would you say in your context fall in that tween category?

Right now, we have an average of probably about 25 that are in the tween category, fifth and sixth grade. We have half of them that are wanting to be on Mountain Movers [worship leadership group] with us, so had about 12 of the 13 of the 25, that are with us in the worship aspect.

So even thinking about a smaller context...because there'll be a lot of people reading this who are in churches that are half of that! Most churches are in that 250 to 400 range, as opposed to the 600 to 1,000 range. But even if you've got 5 to 10 tweens, that observing piece, how do you actually do that? Is it just you observing, and then after every Sunday you're jotting down a few notes? Or is it...do you survey the kids?

You can have job descriptions, for one. It's like, "Here's what we can offer. Here's what we do." So you take a survey and let them fill out what they want to do. You have people help you. In Children's Ministry you should always be working yourself out of a job. You should be giving away your responsibility and your authority as quickly as you can to invest in others.

The other adults there are helping you in this. You're not the only set of eyes. They're going to open up to other people more than they're going to open up to you at times. You want to reach a few, and let other people reach a few. But your other adult leaders are going, "Man, I talked to this kid, and they want to try this drama skit." Or, "I talked to this one, and they have this heart to sing this particular song." It's working at it as a team, and investing in the tweens. It's a team approach.

Ok. Good point. I would imagine in a different context that people are going to be sharing that information differently. Some of them have a weekly team meeting. Other people are sending things out through email. Other people might create a Google doc with a spreadsheet of the kids' names. And when you think of something that a kid would be good at, plop it into the document there. There are so many different ways. But really, the thought that came into my mind was that the observing has to be captured in some way to make sure that it's implemented on.

Yes, it does.

So, we've got S, P, and O. The Scripture, and Purpose and Observation. What's the "I?"

This is probably the hardest part. This is the "Investing" part. This takes the most time. You need to share with them what it is to be a leader. It's not, "Do what you want to do." It's not you getting the spotlight on stage. It's you being the servant. It's you stepping up and taking out the trash, or straightening the chairs, or telling the other kids to be quiet. Or, not taking on the fun roles all the time, but some of the more difficult roles. So investing in them, what a leader is, and what a minister is. Because you're really ministering and leading, and ministering to others.

Then allow them to serve. That's how you're investing in them. Have job descriptions written out. "Here's step by step what I want you to do." Because we're not really allowed to correct anybody, if they don't have the expectations to begin with. You've got to set that expectation first. "Here's what I want you to do." Then if they mess up, you can say, "Well no, I told you what to do. Here's what's expected." Because if not, it wasn't ever their fault to begin with because they didn't know they messed up.

That's the reason you set up that clear expectation to begin with. The job description. You invest in them by having an adult in every area they're serving. So you have a person that's helping them while they're singing on stage. You have another adult at the computer system with them. So they can't fail! It's a win situation for them. You have a contract you have written up with them to invest in saying times they've got to show up and what's expected. Because if they don't come and practice, or they don't know how to do the job they're trained to do, they don't need to be worshiping or leading other kids if they're not prepared. Coach, one-on-one, in leadership.

Then also allow them to share the gospel. Teach them how, not only to receive the gospel, because we teach kids the ABCs. But how do you actually unpack that and share that with another child? How do you share the wordless book as a child to a child? So lead them through that.

Then there's activities you can do inside and outside of the church. Activities inside the church, like cleaning the preschool or nursery toys that nobody ever wants to touch. Let the fifth and sixth graders do that. Or, help pull up weeds outside in the parking lot. Or, cards for shut-ins. Or, pick up clutter around the church, because that always happens. Or, straightening chairs. Or, maybe your machine breaks inside the church and you can't fold bulletins. Have the fifth and sixth graders help fold bulletins. There's a bunch of different jobs inside the church that add up that they can do and be servant leaders inside the church.

Outside the church we've done several things. There's a safe program, stuff animals for emergencies, so we collected stuff animals. Parents were thrilled to get rid of all those goofy stuffed animals at the house. But during a time of emergency for a fire department, a police department, whoever, that gift of a stuffed animal broke the ice. Broke down walls and made the child feed safe. There are snacks for firefighters that have to go out all the time. We've done car washes, tracts, VBS. We did a homeless ministry. So we did homeless packs that we could give homeless people.

But this is the big one that we've done, to invest in them. They serve throughout the year with us inside the church, so once a year we take them on a mission trip. We did this last year at this church. I did it several years at the previous church. We're doing it again this summer. We're going to Gatlinburg, Tennessee. We're going to the different campgrounds to do mini-Vacation Bible Schools and worship services on Sunday. Then go to a couple of the theme parks where they have go-carts and do face painting and balloon animals, and sharing that way. But getting them outside of the church, what they've learned inside the church to reach the world and fulfill the great commission.

That's great. As you were rattling off a whole list of ideas, I think it'd be important for the children's pastor - and if they have a staff, great, or if it's a smaller church and it's just a handful of volunteers, ok – to take their staff and volunteers out to lunch, and just brainstorm. What are the different things that people are doing, or aren't doing, in the church that our fifth and sixth graders could do? What are those?

And even just coming up with that list. That "I" of Investing really circles back to the Observation. If you've got a list of the potential things they could even do, then you're going to be more likely to notice in that Observing phase, a kid that can fit that for sure. Or, just even to bring it up in conversation.

Even simple things like the invitation cards inside the pews or replacing the pencils or pens around chairs that get lost all the time, simple stuff.

Right. Okay. It seems like we've got one more.

One more, it's the "L."

What's the "L?"

"L" is "Love." It's what the Bible says we ought to do, is love one another and that's what we need to do. We do that by…we pray with and for them. We never stop an event – with a fifth and sixth grade group, with what we're doing – without having a prayer time and sharing prayer requests. Do you get monotonous ones like, "My dog's sick?" Yes, you do. It's going to come up. I hurt my pinky. [Laughing] Okay, we got that. But, when you get the ones about, "They're about to take the house," or "My grandmother's dying of cancer," they don't need to be carrying that on their shoulders. But, when you pray for them you see God work, and you can celebrate together. Man, that's loving them.

Correct them is the loving thing to do. It's called discipline. Most people see it as bad. Discipline and correcting is actually a loving way to care for us. God disciplines up because he loves us. We need to correct and help guide the tweens, the fifth and sixth graders. One way to do it is out of loving.

This is a tough one: Allow them to fail. Give them permission to say, "It's okay to mess up. Just do your best. If you mess up we'll work on it." But it's okay of they have a flaw. They're not perfect, they're learning.

Have an adult assigned to each one to help when needed. That's loving. Send cards in the mail, and emails to them. Just to say, "Hey, I'm thinking about you. Praying for you this week. Thanks for serving," goes a long way. Because they never get mail. They never get attention from others outside their family. Visit their church activity, or their outside activities from church. If they're in sports or whatever. Go to a dance recital. Go to whatever they're in and visit them outside the church.

Then quarterly, we have an event just for our tweens. It's nothing but fellowship. Last week we went bowling. We've taken them to the movies. We go play putt-putt. We go to a corn maze. Some activity just for them that nobody else can go to. And then you brag about it! "Hey, don't forget about the fifth and sixth grade event." The kids will go, "Why can't we go do that?" "Well, you're not to the sixth grade yet. You're not a tween. When you become a tween we'll take you." So it gives them something for the younger kids to look forward to.

The last two things are really important. One is Bible study. Have a short Bible study. Even if it's just going over a scripture with them and unpacking it. To allow them to go deeper and understand on their level. Then the last one is encourage, encourage, encourage. Never stop pouring into them! For every time you correct them, you ought to be pouring in three times of encouragement, and just telling them how important they are. So you just love on them. If you S.P.O.I.L. them, they're going to turn around and spoil you with great leadership.

That's a great place to end. If we S.P.O.I.L. them with Scripture and Purpose, and Observing them, and Investing in them and Loving them, they will turn around and spoil us with great leadership. That's fantastic. Thank you so much, Stanley. I'm looking forward to sharing this with a lot of people.

Thank you. It's been a pleasure.

Stanley Mearse

Stanley Mearse is a Children's Minister from Hickory, North Carolina, has been serving the Lord in ministry to children and families for the past 18 years. He earned a Bachelor in Elementary Education and a Masters of Divinity. His favorite place to teach is in the church where he is able to build relationships and disciple families.

How do I lay a solid foundation as a NEW family ministry leader?

I'm here with Kathie Phillips. Thank you so much for joining me today.

Thanks for having me, Keith.

I'm so excited to hear your insight on building that solid foundation specifically for the new kidmin leader. Before we do, give us a little bit of context. What's been your children's ministry journey and what context do you serve in now?

Sure. I started out in children's ministry as a teenager in high school. Then I went off to college and continued ministering in children's ministry where I was, there in Virginia. And then I got married and had my own two children. They became my full-time children's ministry for 10 years! Then I was hired at a local church here in the Baltimore area to oversee their children's program birth through fifth grade.

I was there for about five years. It was a smaller church; we averaged about 60 adults and about 25-30 children each week. After five years there, I was hired at my current church where I now oversee birth through fifth grade here at Central Presbyterian Church in Baltimore. So that's what I'm doing now.

Great, great. Now, we're going to look at a lot of the "how" of building this foundation. I've heard you go so far as to say that building that solid foundation for the new kidmin leader is the key to your ministry's success longterm. So, unpack a little bit of the "why" before we dive into the "how."

Sure. I think that having a strong foundation as a new kidmin leader is so important because it really drives everything that you do as the leader of your children's ministry – from your mission, your vision, your core values. All of that filters through the programming that you choose to do. Your curriculum that you select, the events and outreach things that you opt to do, it all should funnel through those key pieces like the mission, vision, and values. I think having that foundation set at the beginning will help the whole ministry really fall into place and be cohesive.

Indeed. Now, let's say that you are sitting in a coffee shop with somebody who has just gotten their first kidmin leader job, whether that be a significant volunteer position or a staff position. What are some practical things that new kidmin leader can do to get started on a solid foundation and build that ministry foundation?

I think one of the most important things to do is to learn the church culture of where you'll be serving, whether you're in a new church environment or a church you have been a part of for a while. I think it's important to actually learn the culture of your church. And by that I mean: What are the things that are important to your church? Is your church intergenerational in mindset? Is it a church with older adults? Is it a church of young families? Is it a church of millennials? Get to learn the culture of the church where you serve, because I think a lot of that will also play into some of that success that you have in your ministry.

By learning the culture, I would suggest that you ask questions. Ask a lot of questions! Ask about policies that are in place. Ask why these particular policies and procedures are in place. Because there's a reason why. As the new leader it's important for you to understand why those things are in place.

Along with that, get to learn the cultures; get to know the people. So whether you are overseeing staff, or teams, or volunteers...get to know them! Talk to them about what they feel is working well, and what they feel could be improved. So I think asking questions and listening is very important in the beginning.

And then, after that, all kinds of assessments have been made. Then I would suggest praying about the next steps: What needs to be changed immediately (especially if it's a safety issue)? Like, are there any things that need to be addressed immediately? I would definitely assess that and get a team of people around you to help. First things first, what are we going to do first to really map out a strategy for that?

Ask questions, listen, get to know your people, and just pray and ask God for discernment on what strategy you should take to really get your footing sure as the new leader.

I love that idea of asking questions and listening. I think, the challenge a new leader has – whether it's a kidmin role, or a youthmin role, or a new pastor, or a new job in the corporate world – is so often the person is so excited about the job and so excited to move forward that they come in with all their ideas of what's going to happen.

As I've talked to people about this, and experienced it myself when I was first a youth pastor, I think the light bulb for me went on a little bit as you were talking about even looking at the policies and then asking why those policies are there. I think that's something that's not intuitively done, not something that people naturally go, "Oh, you know what? I'm new to this job. I want to look at the policies." But that can tell you so much about the culture, especially if you approach those with an attitude of listening.

Yeah, and I think that the excitement of being new, you come in and you just want to make change. Or you want to put your personal stamp on things. But I think it's important to talk to those people who are invested in the ministry currently, and hear from them. You definitely don't want to offend any of your volunteers by coming in and doing something just to make it different and new.

So I think there is definitely some value in waiting, listening, discerning, before moving forward with any kind of sweeping change. Because you really want them to buy in to you as the leader and the direction that God has called you to take the ministry in. You definitely want the buy-in for that. And part of that is valuing those people who have been a part of the ministry. I think that definitely honors them.

Yes! Honoring the people who not only have gone before, but people who were there before and are still there.

Right, absolutely. Absolutely!

And with the previous children's pastor...I think it's certainly great if you can talk positively about that person for sure.

Right.

I think we forget that, that the people who are your volunteers initially are likely people that have been volunteering in that ministry for a long time.

Right, right, and you certainly don't want to offend them by coming in and undoing all of the things they have in place without finding out why they are in place. So I think starting that dialogue helps them to know you're not only concerned about the ministry, but also that you value them and their opinion.

I'd love to get your insight. We didn't talk specifically about this question, so sorry in advance for putting you on the spot here.

Okay.

But I'd love to hear your thoughts. You've had two different roles, different churches – in addition to the volunteering that you've done – two different staff roles, and lead roles. What would you tell that new kidmin leader, as you're sitting in that coffee shop, about them staying spiritually healthy and even physically healthy? What are the spiritual practices that you would recommend them putting into place from the get-go, and maybe what are the boundaries that you would encourage them to establish so that they can prepare for not just doing this for a year or two but for a decade or two?

I think that's a great question. One of the things that I'd definitely recommend is to pace yourself. Not all of the things, have to be done at once. So you bring that energy, that excitement with you, and you want to sustain that over the long haul, so I think that recognizing that all of the things that you might want to do and change and incorporate don't have to be done in the first month or two or three that you're there. Some of those things might take years to do. It's important for a healthy leader to pace yourself. All of it doesn't have to be done in a short period of time.

Along with that, I would say to definitely keep a Sabbath. I know that's really hard to do, but those times off are so important for you as a leader to refresh, renew yourself, reenergize yourself. For the upcoming weekend, if you take it before your weekend programming, or on the back-end if you take it after the weekend program. But you do need to have that time for you to get rest, have hobbies, have lunch with a friend, or take a nap or read or do a personal retreat day. Those things are definitely important to prioritize.

If you have a struggle with that, I would say ask someone to keep you accountable. Someone who can ask you, "Have you done this?" And then put it in your calendar as a to-do item. To do nothing! We need to give ourselves permission to do nothing. That helps keep us balanced.

Also I would suggest that you find a network of like-minded ministry leaders. That has been a valuable gift to me. I am a part of a local children's ministry leader's network. We meet quarterly just to get together. We share ideas, we do many training sessions, we learn from each other. Some of my greatest support ministry ideas have come from that local face-to-face gathering. And then I also have friends from around the country that we get on Skype and we pray for each other and we text back and forth. So I think having that kind of support is definitely invaluable to you as a leader.

Yeah, invaluable! Doing ministry in community is so vital. And I like what you mentioned about finding people within your city, within your network. Because oftentimes, that sense of community can't necessarily be found within your own church, because you're the one that's doing it! To find people that are like-minded, means they're probably doing it somewhere else.

Right, and I'm not necessarily sure even that it should be people in their church. I don't think it should necessarily be your key leaders. I think that that has its place. But I think for you to grow as a leader, you need to have a safe place outside of that sphere of influence to be able to share some of the things that you might not be able to share within your church context. I think that's very important.

Yeah, I think so too. And the Sabbath you mentioned earlier. Just last week, I was at a conference where somebody was speaking on the Sabbath and saying that it is one of the easiest to understand and the most broken of the commands in Scripture.

Yes. It's one of the easier things to let go because our to-do lists are always long. We always have something that we should be doing or could be doing, and so it's easier to push the Sabbath off so that we can check it off the list. But in the long-term, it's just not a good practice. So whatever fills your cup up are definitely things that you should do for your Sabbath.

Indeed.

Honor it as much as you can.

Absolutely. I have a former pastor friend of mine who said taking off the Sabbath was equal parts him resting and also being reminded that God can continue to do ministry when we're not producing anything.

Right, right.

He said the more consistent he was in his Sabbath, the more trusting he was of God's goodness and faithfulness.

Yeah, and really set up good boundaries around your Sabbath about answering email or not answering email or texts or things like that. You want to be intentional about protecting that time as much as you can.

In addition to that, also protect your vacation time. Take vacation! I know so many leaders who do not take vacation because they feel like if they aren't there, things are going to fall apart. And they may, but it's okay. It'll be okay. So you have to give yourself permission to pull away and protect that time, because you need that for the long haul.

We've covered a lot of ground! From listening and starting strong and policies and volunteers and Sabbath. Thank you so much for taking the time to do this, and blessings on your ministry as well.

Thank you so much.

Kathie Phillips

Kathie Phillips currently serves as the Director of Children's Ministry at a church in Baltimore, Maryland. In addition, she's a wife, mom of two young adults, conference speaker, ministry coach, published author and blogger.

DR. KAYLA PRAY

How do I create space in my ministry for my kids' emotions?

I'm here today with Dr. Kayla Pray. Thank you so much for joining me.

Happy to.

Set some context for somebody who may not know you. What's been your journey in children's ministry? What context have you served in and what context are you in right now?

I grew up in a medium sized church. There were probably about 400 kids that go to their VBS. I started there when I was about 13 years old teaching a kindergarten class, which then turned into me running a children's choir, which then turned into me sponsoring and chaperoning summer trips to different places. And so, from 13 on, I've always worked with children. Going through my youth group, working with the kids. And then when I got out of youth group, started actually working with the youth group, which is when I started counseling. So right about 19, I began mentoring and life coaching young girls.

And then it grew into this counseling ministry that God has called me into. I've been in private practice counseling now for four years, but I still continue to serve at my church. There are several churches I work with. I go in and I teach youth conferences. I still run VBS. I'm still the "music lady," and I have been since I was 14. So, most of the kids in town know me either from music or from church ministry. I go and speak at youth conferences. I do training for children's ministry pastors, as well as the bigger conferences. Just teaching about ministry and counseling and emotions and how to best serve these kids.

Good. You use that word "emotions." I know one of the phrases that is one of your hallmarks is this idea of "creating space for emotions." Now, before we get into how to do that, what do you even mean by creating space for emotions?

What I mean by "creating space" starts with remembering that emotions are synonymous with children. You think of tantrums in the toddler stages. And then behavioral problems up into the elementary. And then the rebellious teenage streak going into the teen years. And all of that is just basically emotions. They're angry. They're sad. They're grumpy. They're difficult. They're irrational.

Therefore, creating space for the emotions really is allowing the emotions to "be" in the appropriate ages…and not disciplining the emotion. Learning to let children have emotions. To cope with the emotions, and not always being in trouble because of their emotions.

I work with a lot of kids, and I say, "Well, what happened at school?" "I got in trouble." "Well, why'd you get in trouble?" "Because I got angry." There's this association with anger as the problem and not their behavior.

That's what I mean by "creating space." Let the emotions be. Then we can talk about behavior and obedience and godliness as separate from the emotional implications.

Okay. That's good. So, and this may seem like an obvious question, but I'd like you to unpack it a little bit. Why do you see this as needed for children? In children in general, but then specifically in the Church context? Is it something that's not being done? Is it something we've never even thought of?

I think it's something that people desire to do, and it's one of those things that when I say it out loud, when I do a training or when I talk to a parent or a ministry professional about creating space for emotions, they're kind of like, "Oh yeah. That would be needed. That's good."

But there's this lack of "how to." There is a lack of identifying what it is. Particularly because when you're dealing with children and emotions in a church setting, think of your average nine-year-old. He has been at school all week or all day. Being told what to do by all these other people. So, by the time he actually gets to his children's minister, he's a little crazy. He's tired of listening to adults. He's tired of doing things. And so, his emotions are high.

Moreover, that is not really the atmosphere where it's easy to then take a step back as the adult and go, "I wonder what's going on here? I wonder how I can create space?" Because you've got a lesson to get through. You've got a craft going on. You've got parents coming through the door asking questions.

It just becomes this, "I need you to behave. I need you to listen. I need you to…" and then we're back to focusing on behavior. So, I don't think it's an intentional that we're not going to give space. I think it gets lost in the shuffle. I think that's what is happening for most church ministries I've worked with and for most people I talked to. Nobody wants to stifle emotions, but I think that's what accidentally happens.

As far as why the kids need it? They've done studies, and it's proven that children feel emotions to the same extent that adults do. A 30-year-old individual feels anger quite strongly. But the difference is, I have coping skills. I have filters in my brain. I have maturity to understand that anger.

A nine-year-old has no coping skills. So, he's going to feel anger to the same extent I feel it with no help, no benefit. And this is where we get tantrums. This is where we get the behavioral problems. And so, they don't know what to do with this emotion. It just suddenly is there and it's upon them and it takes over their brain.

I liken it to a blood pressure cuff on the arm. And it just gets tighter and tighter and tighter. You and I know, "Oh, if I just turn this little valve, it all goes away." The child has no knowledge of that, they're just maintaining in this emotional state. Until eventually, they do blow, something has to give. I think that's partly why it's needed, because they don't know what to do with it.

Also, we live in such a tech-filled world. Now, I have nothing against technology. But I have the coping skills to manage and maintain my technology, and so, if I'm watching a show and it's been lots of drama and it's been lots of explosions and my emotions are peaked, I know I need a break. I need to go be quiet. Again, kids don't have that filter, and they're exposed to so much tech like that that triggers their emotions, and there's no space for that emotion to manifest or to be. I really think that's why it's needed in ministry and in homes.

Okay so, that's great. What would you say is the place to start for a children's pastor or volunteer team whose interest is now peaked, and they say, "Yes, we want to be a church and environment where we create that space for emotions?" How do they start, and what are those half-a-dozen practical steps they can take? What could they do?

That's where it always comes back to with kids, we can agree that children are balls of emotion, I like to say, "This is a person unrefined." Eventually this will be a logical, thinking individual, but right now they're completely unrefined. Those leadership skills are coming out in angry, controlling outbursts. That sensitivity and that empathy is coming out in weeping over everything. Everyone can agree kids are just these emotional beings. But what do we do with them? How do we guide it? How do we?

In most cases, what ends up happening is we either go to stoicism, which is where you just don't have emotions. You're governing the emotions as if they were behaviors. Johnny got angry, and so he hit a friend, and now Johnny's in trouble. And no one goes back and tells Johnny, "The reason you're in trouble is because you hit your friend. Not because you got angry." Eventually Johnny will learn to just not have emotions. He just shuts them down, because emotions always get him in trouble.

And then the other side of that is you end up with a child who's just irrational. "My emotions are constantly giving me a problem. So then, I'm just going to give into all of my emotions. They're just going to be the thing that guides me. I give up trying to be good."

A "how to" place to start is having that education with children about what an emotion is. In children's ministry or for a children's pastor, you've got 45 kids on Wednesday night. And you know you've got four of them who just are always having these outbursts. This is where you tell your staff and your volunteers, "Okay, if Johnny does something because he's angry, we pull him aside and we don't address his behavior yet. We ask, "What's going on tonight? You seem upset." And then we start teaching about are you angry? Are you frustrated? Letting him vent that feeling. After he's vented the feeling, "Yeah, today was just really hard at school." Or, I live in a military town, so often it's, "Well, Dad was deployed today." There's an emotion there that they came in with.

Once they've been able to vent that, "I'm just really angry tonight," "Okay, but we don't hit our friends when we're angry. You can't do that. What do you think would be a better thing to do when you're angry?" It just starts this education piece, really. And once mastered, once everyone knows that's what they're supposed to do, it doesn't take that long. It really is about 30 to 60 seconds, about the time it would take you to discipline him for hitting his friend.

Right.

That's where I want everyone to start when I come into these consulting areas and I work with parents and ministers. Educate him about the emotion. What did he do in his emotion that was wrong, but not that the emotion was bad? So, that's a quick way to verbally create space. As far as a group setting, if you have those 45 kids, make emotions something that you naturally talk about. Share something personal. Like, "I was really sad today because my dog is sick," or something. And it's just a quick thing, "Today was very exciting for me because I got a free pizza coupon." And the kids can start relating to you in those emotional ways, rather than just the academic, logical ways that we normally go to as defaults.

I liked that idea of letting the emotion be the starting point as opposed to the behavior. What, and this is kind of on the fly, we didn't talk about this ahead of time.

Okay. I'm good with that.

Are there any other either phrases that are good for volunteers? When you're training a team on that, are there some phrases that you say that are good entry points?

So, phrases I like to teach them, there's a lot of what not to say. Like, "Why did you do that?" They [the kid] don't know.

Right.

You're going to get an honest, "I don't know." They don't know why they did it, so that's kind of a wasted question. And so they've already picking up on your tone in that question, "Oh, you're mad at me now. And I don't know how to answer you." So, instead of saying, "Why did you do that," you pull them aside, you go, "What's going on?" That's the one I like, is "What's going on?" Because then they get to give you an answer. And it's not a yes/no; kind of the child looking at you like, "What do you want from me?" Which is often what they get with a "why" question.

With a "why," they're assuming there's a correct answer here, and I need to know what it is. If you say, "What's going on?" I can give you facts. "Well, he pushed me, then I just got angry, so I pushed him back." Or, "I just don't like it when we play this game." You start getting to the root of what's bothering them. I like the phrase, "What's going on?"

And most kids will respond to that. If you get an "I don't know," then they're just still kind of more sullen. And I give the kids space then. I'm like, "Okay, well, why don't you go stand by Ms. So-and-So, and think about what's going on. Because you don't seem happy and you don't seem like your normal self."

Again, we're going after that emotion of, "This doesn't seem like you, let's go take some time and think about what's going on."

Good. Good. This has been great. As I'm having this conversation with you, I feel like this is the tip of the iceberg.

Yes.

I think the overwhelming feeling for me is that this is the starting place. As we venture into that scary space of actually having the emotion conversations, those will lead to more comfort with it and we'll kind of find our own phrases that work for our context.

Yes. And what I often come up against is people don't want to have the emotion conversations, because we as adults are not comfortable talking about our own emotions. I don't really want to talk to Johnny about his emotions when I'm not comfortable sharing mine. This is why it's easier for us as adults just to go to logic, to go to behavior, to go to the tasks. "I can see that you punched your friend and I can address that." It's harder for me to see your anger. It's harder for me to see your fear and your sadness. I have to get comfortable in that realm of dealing with my emotions and the emotions of the other adults around me, and then teach this child how to be comfortable with his emotions.

And that's what I mean, we either go to stoicism or the irrationality. Either don't have emotion or completely give into the emotions. And that's not how God designed us. We serve an emotional God. He has feelings. He has these emotions. The emotions are not a problem. It's the behaviors within the problem, how they manifest. And that's what we need to teach kids.

That's why I guess I'm more passionate about creating the space for the emotion.

Good. Thank you for giving us that insight. My hope, my prayer, is that as people read this or watch this interview, that they will enter into becoming comfortable with being uncomfortable. And serving kids there.

Yes.

Thank you so much for taking the time.

You're welcome. Thank you for asking me.

Dr. Kayla Pray

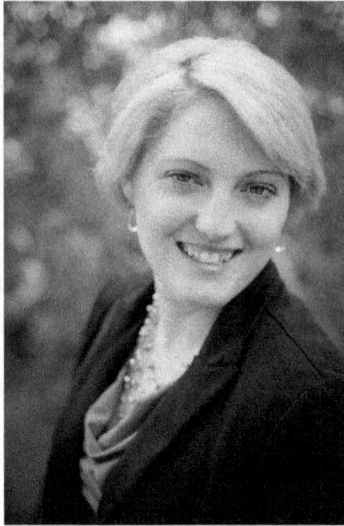

Kayla is a Christian counselor using the best of psychology with Biblical foundations and perspectives. She seeks to help families and individuals lead fulfilling lives. She specializes in Marriage and Family therapy and Child and Adolescent therapy. She has a Master of Arts in Clinical Christian Counseling and a Ph.D. in Clinical Christian Counseling.

How do I create a partnership with parents?

I'm here today with Rob Rienow. Thank you so much for being here, Rob.

Hey Keith, thanks for having me.

And I'm excited to explore this idea of how to best partner with parents. But before we do, what has been your ministry journey so far and what context do you serve in now?

When I was a high school student, my youth pastor played a huge role in my life. And so I felt like God was calling me into youth ministry. I jumped into being a youth pastor right out of college at Wheaton Bible Church, in Wheaton, IL.

I served for 10 years in youth ministry and then transitioned into family ministry where I was overseeing all ministries birth through age 18. I had my children's ministry team serving with me and my task was to help develop a comprehensive discipleship strategy for the next generation. A big emphasis for us was partnering with parents, partnering with the home.

Then, seven years ago, I left full-time pastoring to launch Visionary Family Ministries. Now we are on the road every other weekend doing

Visionary Parenting Conferences, Visionary Marriage Conferences, and training youth and children's ministry leaders around the world with this theology and model of partnering with parents.

That's great. Both you and I have already used that phrase "partnering with parents." Now that I've known you for the better part of a decade, I know this is such a passion for you. How did that become a passion for you and why does it continue to be your passion?

Well, the first 10 years of my ministry life, I was a youth pastor as I said. Amy and I were married and we had four children those first 10 years. My heart and my passion was passing my faith to other people's kids. So I would pray with other people's kids and read the Bible with other people's kids. I'd take other people's kids on retreats.

It was a great season of ministry, but I was neglecting my own family; neglecting my own kids. I wasn't praying with them or reading the Bible with them, and I didn't have any plan to shepherd and disciple them.

In 2004, God brought me to a deep place of repentance and brokenness and turned my heart to the ministry of my family. And then all these Scriptures about how parents should shepherd their kids at home led me to "professional repentance" or "pastoral repentance." Because, if God wants me to shepherd my kids at home, then He wants all the other parents at our church to shepherd their kids at home.

As a youth pastor, I'd been basically saying, "Hey drop your kids off to me and I'll disciple them for you." Now, I didn't say it quite that crassly, but that was sometimes implied. That sent me down this journey of, "If God wants parents to be the primary spiritual trainers of their children in the home?" then, "What would it look like for the church to equip them for spiritual success? How can we unite the church and the family in the great commission to reach the next generation?"

Absolutely vital! I feel like the people reading this book or watching this interview, are people who, for the most part, are sold on the principal of partnering with parents. But they might not necessarily know how or how to get started. Or even how to make that most effective.

So let's spend most of our time unpacking that a bit. Let's start with the simplest idea. What's the most basic place somebody could start if

they really want to put this principal of "partnering with parents" into action in their church?

One of things you've probably heard if you've been around the family ministry world at all is that family ministry is not a program. It's a philosophy, it's a theology, it's an approach.

That's all well and good except what we do as church leaders is run programs! We do stuff. And so that sort of leaves us in this fog. I would suggest to you that there is a program that you've got to run if you want to have a family ministry model, if you want to have a parent partnership model.

And the program you've got to run is family worship in every home. Now family worship is the old fashioned phrase for "family devotions." Family worship is a time when parents pray and read the Bible with their children at home.

Deuteronomy 6 says, "Love the Lord your God with all your heart, with all your soul, with all your strength. These commandments I give to you today are to be upon your hearts. Impress them on your children and talk about them when you sit at home." Talk about the Word of God when you sit at home with your family!

So, right there in the great commandment it's love God. And then –okay parents and grandparents– talk about God with your kids at home. So, the place to start with your team is to say, "How can we get the maximum number of parents and grandparents to start praying and reading the Bible with their kids at home?"

Let me tell you about the first tweak that we made at our church to try to get that going. For years, we had been sending home a piece of paper after Sunday School class. A parent would pick up little Johnny after 3rd Grade class, and they'd get a piece of paper saying, "Today in Sunday School, we learned about prayer. And if you're a good parent (OK we didn't really say that part) you'll go home and read this verse with your child and talk about these questions."

You've probably passed out papers like that before or sent emails. Sadly, however, if there's a trash can outside the room, they might end up in there, or maybe under the seat in the car. Too few parents were using them!

The spirit of the paper is really good! The spirit of the paper is, "We want to communicate to parents what we're doing in the classroom and we would love for parents to follow up and carry the momentum of Sunday School forward." The spirit is good but the theology is terrible. The theology is that Sunday School is the primary trainer and the parent is the reinforcer. The parent is the support. That's upside down and backwards! The Bible says that the parents are the primary spiritual trainers and the Sunday School – or whatever the child is getting at church – should be reinforcement to the home.

So here's what we did. We took next week's paper and sent it home this week. Up on top, we simply wrote, "Take the lead. Next week in Sunday School, we're going to talk about prayer. Here's the scripture that we're going to read. Would you please read this scripture with your kids at home this week? Talk about these three questions. And next week in Sunday School we're going to reinforce the message that they heard from you."

One of the things that we say at our church is, "We don't ever want your kids to hear something at church they haven't first heard from you." Well, how are we going to pull that off? We've got to take what we're doing at church and send it home before we do in the coming weeks so the parents can be primary.

One of my mentors named Ben Freudenberg has a great phrase, he says, "For 1900 years, when it came to reaching kids, the church was home-centered and church-supported. Home first, church second. But in the 20th century, we flipped that around. Now we're church-centered, even church-building-centered, and then home-supported. The job of the family is to support the Sunday School. The job of the family is to support the youth group. It's church first, home second."

We need to return to looking through the lens of home first, church second. Put the lens over the VBS you're doing this summer. Send your VBS curriculum home a month early! Let all the parents see the scriptures and the themes so that the parents can start with some conversations at home and then the church becomes the reinforcer.

Part B to my question is as I'm talking to more and more family ministry folks, one of the specific challenges of today's day-and-age is that a lot of the kids who are in their children's ministry are going home to parents who either weren't at church or to parents who were never discipled and maybe don't even know how to have these conversations. What would you suggest is the church's responsibility to become the support of what's happening at home if there's nothing happening at home? Or if the people at home don't even know how to start?

Right. You mentioned two groups there. One, you mentioned immature Christians; Christian parents who may not be thriving in their faith. They probably did not come from a family that discipled them. But then you also mentioned the kid in your children's ministry whose parents don't even go to church. They don't have Christian parents.

Our strategies with those two groups are going to be different. Let's start with the nominal church parent. They are not thriving in their faith and so we ask, "How in the world are they going to disciple their kids when they're not even growing in their faith?" This is the task of the church!

Part of the task of the church is Ephesians 4:13, "To equip the saints for works of ministry." And if you've got a child, if you've got a son or daughter, your great commission ministry begins with them. So your Sunday School or your children's ministry has such a powerful opportunity to actually disciple the parent! Because what you are doing in children's ministry is basic Christian discipleship. You're teaching kids, obviously, you're trying to get the basic doctrines of the Bible, the basic applications of the Christian faith, but what better curriculum to put in the hands of a parent who may be a new Christian who hasn't been discipled themselves?

You're on the front lines. They probably interact with your ministry more than any other ministry in the church. So you're casting vision for them to say, "Hey, no matter where you are in your spiritual life, your number one calling from God is to help your kids follow Jesus."

My friend Greg Braly gave me this phrase from his children's ministry approach, "We want to be your best friend and your greatest support on your parenting journey." That's the job of our children's ministry when it comes to parents. We want to be your best friend and greatest support on your parenting journey.

We are going to train you. We're going to equip you. You may feel insecure. You may feel like you don't know Genesis from the maps in the back. You open the Bible and you don't know what's going on. But we're going to help you.

Now let's talk about the other group. You say, "Well Rob, I've got some kids in my children's ministry who don't even have Christian parents. So how in the world is this whole family ministry thing going to work for them?"

Here's what's happening in churches that are really catching hold of the family discipleship theology. A about the five-year mark: More and more of the Christian parents of all spectrums are starting to play the primary role of the discipler in the home.

The child has family worship in the home. The child is participating in the corporate worship service at the church. They're getting their spiritual meals at home and at church. Sunday School is becoming less critical for their spiritual development. The Sunday School is becoming a vitamin because they're already getting their meals at home so they're less dependent on that one hour of the week.

And here's what happens for those in the children's ministry; the children's ministry pastor and the children's ministry workers increasingly spend more of their time and strategy on kids who don't have Christian parents.

The dirty little secret is this, 80% of what we do in most children's ministry is basic Christian discipleship for church kids. It is most of what we do! Now you've got some non-Christian kids there, and we're trying. We're trying to do outreaches. We're trying to give special attention, but we're so overwhelmed with doing basic discipleship for the regular church-going kids, that our strategy's always peripheral for these kids who don't have Christian parents.

For churches that get a hold of home discipleship, of family discipleship, what happens is that attention flips. 80% of the attention of children's ministry and youth ministry is for the kids who don't have Christian parents. I love that!

Yeah. Absolutely! Now, we've looked at a little bit of the why, looked at some ideas for how to shift even our mindset when it comes to how we think about programs, and looked at different, let's say, "categories" of parents. So, what if somebody's reading this and says, "I love this. I am fully onboard. I absolutely believe this is true. My volunteers agree with me. But I'm getting zero support from my lead pastor or my church council or board of elders."

What do they do? And maybe that would lead into the second part of how do you help somebody else catch this vision?

The first thing is that you do what you can in your own sphere. For example, that idea we talked about earlier; take next week's paper and send it home this week. I hope you don't need board approval to do that.

First, get that done. Then, let's say you do a Wednesday night children's ministry of some kind. What if the first Wednesday of every quarter was a family night? We would call it a "generations night." It's not a drop-your-kid-off-and-leave night. It's stay all together and we're all going to sing together, we're all going to play the games together and we're all going to do the lesson together.

Again, I think that's sort of a simple tweak. But you may be thinking, "Wow! Every quarter? That'd be too much." Okay, then once a year. Make some small tweak of your programming to get the generations together.

Now, big picture wise, there are lot of churches that are doing some great stuff in family ministry. But the reason they're able to do it is because they have one person on staff who's got a bee in their bonnet about this thing and they've got some influence and so they're making it happen.

But if that person were to leave the staff, then all that family ministry would go with them. Because the reason that church is doing it, isn't because it's built in to the doctrine of the church, it's built into that person.

And so, as you work with the rest of your staff, here's what I would encourage you to do. Make an appointment with your senior pastor. The meeting goes something like this…

"Hey I could really use your help over the next 12 months. I have been wrestling with how we can better equip parents, how can we better partner with parents, and how the church and the home can work together for the gospel. I don't want to just go off and do my thing or do stuff that I think is a good idea. Could we spend some time over the next 12 months (maybe with the elders, pastors, or whatever your church leadership structure looks like) and you could help me put together a one-page "theology of family" for our church? I would like some Scriptures that address:

Why did God make the family?

What does God say to parents in the Bible?

What does God say about marriages in the Bible?

How does that link to the Great Commission?

Because if I had a theological base from the elders, from the pastors, I could then come back to you all and say, 'How are we living this out in our church? How could we hilp parents? How could we help families do this?' But I need that Scriptural base to build this stuff on so I'm not just off doing whatever I want."

Now we've had a lot of folks do that with their senior pastors and I'll say 9 out of 10 times, there's great enthusiasm for that. You're asking your senior pastor to help you lead with a theological base and they love it! And truthfully, and I don't mean to be too harsh here, but if you go to your senior pastor and you ask for 12 months, a couple of meetings, some thought and some emails on a one page document, if he's not inclined to give his time to help you do that, it might be time to start praying about another opportunity somewhere for you. Because you're not getting an ounce of theological leadership from above.

Right. That may be a good spot to wrap up. That this idea of family ministry and partnering with parents is not just a principal or even a practical application, but it's also somewhat of a barometer for discernment asking, "Am I in a place of doing effective ministry?"

If it is a place that doesn't celebrate and affirm and equip people to partner with parents – one of the most clear and vital commands in the Bible – then that is an area of discernment as well.

I think you and I could talk about this for hours and, well, in fact we have for the last 10 years! Thanks for sharing your time and your wisdom and I look forward to the next time you and I are in the same room together.

I'm excited too Keith. Thanks.

Dr. Rob Rienow

Dr. Rob Rienow's most important ministry is loving his wife Amy and partnering with her to lead their seven children to love God. He is the founder of Visionary Family Ministries (VisionaryFam.com), a pastor, international conference speaker, and the author of several books including Visionary Parenting and Visionary Marriage. When Rob is not fishing for men, he enjoys fishing for fish. The Rienow family lives in West Chicago, IL.

How do I develop and execute a ministry plan?

Hey Jason, thanks so much for being here today.

My pleasure, Keith. Good to be here.

Before we dive into this massive, really important topic of having a ministry plan, give us a little bit of a background on your ministry journey, and the context you serve in now.

I started off in a drama ministry, traveling around the world with a ministry team doing performing arts for people in different environments - churches, non-profits, and conventions, things like that. From there I transitioned into children's ministry. Started as like a children's worship leader, designing worship experiences for kids, and then went into curriculum development for a while, overseeing a curriculum called Elevate that we created out of our church.

And from there I went and worked for an international ministry creating a digital product, an online world where kids could engage in God's Word wherever they are and whenever they wanted to. And so from there we started looking at how can we address technological, cultural challenges the church is facing and help ministries to work through that, and thrive in those environments.

And that ministry is called Ministry Accelerator?

Yeah, Ministry Accelerator.

That's great. So, this idea of a ministry plan, maybe we should just start with the "why." Why do you feel that it's important to have a ministry plan for a children's pastor? Obviously, church vision is one thing, but why is it important to have it, and do you think most people do?

I think it's important to have it because you have a group of people that are the future generations of the church, that start in your nursery and may leave your elementary program, and the question is: What do you want them to know? What do you want them to be when they leave? How do you want them to change?

We find out that most kids accept Christ before the age of 14. That makes you the one reaching the most under-reached people group in your church at any given time. So you most definitely need a plan, because otherwise, how do you know what you're accomplishing? What measurements do you have? You can't use something like attendance, because attendance is all over the map nowadays. You can possibly use baptisms, if your church does some form of baptisms, or professions. But do you really know what your kids are experiencing and how their growing in Christ and becoming disciples as a result of their time with you?

And we found out that a lot of people don't. We did a survey in 2016, and we found out 51% of people said they don't have any plan for their kids' spiritual development as they come to their ministry. Now the funny thing was, 92% of them said they believe their children left their ministry as mature disciples. The question is, "How do they know this?"

So, when you think about all the things that a ministry does, and you really can look at a children's ministry as a microcosm of exactly what the church does. They teach kids worship. They teach kids how to live in a community with one another and be the church relationally. They help introduce people to the Gospel, most of them for the first time. If children are not learning about God in their homes, it's happening in the children's ministry. They help them on their first steps towards spiritual maturity. When you have all those things taking place, and you're putting all your energies into programming your weekend, or your summer events, or your discipleship groups, and you don't have a plan... How do you know you're putting your energies in the right place? How do you know you're giving your kids what they need?

So, let's just start from the very beginning. What is the first step? You know, if you were sitting down right now, and a children's pastor said, "You know what? I don't have a plan, and I don't really know where to start." What's the plan?

Yeah, that's good. The first question I think that I would encourage the pastor to ask himself is, "What does a mature child coming out of my ministry look like? What kind of fruit do they exhibit? What kind of relationships do they have? What are the things they know about scripture? What are the things they know about God?" What are those things that they knew that when they leave, this is what they're equipped with? Begin with the end in mind. You want to know what you're aiming for. From there, I would suggest that once they answer that question for themselves, back up and say, "How do I get that into a child?"

As you think of the plans that you developed, and the plans you've helped other people develop, what are the core elements? Obviously, each children's pastor is going to have some differences-

Sure.

But what are the core elements that you see as the universal places to at least get those "pillars," if you will, to make sure that they have a good plan?

I like that term ... You used the term "pillars." I want to go back to that in a minute, because, actually, we call them "legs of a stool." But I'll get to that in just a second. You want to know, you want to think through theologically what a child needs to learn What do they know about Jesus and the Gospel? What do they know about God and their place in relation to God? What do they know about the Holy Spirit and His work in the world? How do they see what God is doing and how they fit into that. So their image, their value, their worth, and how their worth is separate from what they do.

Especially in America, we have such a performance-based society. Where kids s are worrying about their performance so much younger.

They put their value in their performance. We want to make sure that they know their value comes from who they are and who redeemed them. Not from what they do.

You, want them to understand the basic stories of the Bible, and how those fit into God's good picture for our life. So, from Creation to Revelation, you want to talk about not just how God did these things, but how He's redeeming the world and their role in it. You might think, "Well that's a bit over a kid's head." In some cases, that's the point! You want the kids to work out their faith.!

And that also changes based on, I mean, somebody reading this book is may only be responsible for kindergarten through fifth grade.

Right.

Other people reading this book, in their context, they're responsible from cradle all the way up through high school.

Right.

And so, how you answer that question and whether it's over somebody's head definitely is evaluated context by context. But it's absolutely an important question.

And that's the thing, it's important to define it. To have something that you say, "This is what we're trying to accomplish."

Right.

The other thing I think you should define closely is what "channels" you're going to use. That's where the term "three-legged stool" comes into play. I've always said, "To me, children's ministry is a three-legged stool, because if you don't invest in these three legs, the stool doesn't stand up."

The first leg is children. You've got to invest in how you're reaching children. The second leg is the parents of those children, because they're the first pastors of the kids. I heard a pastor in Latin America use that phrase, and I loved it. He said, "They're the first pastors of the children." And I'm thinking, "Yes! They are the first shepherds of these children." So you have to invest and equip in them. The third leg is any influential adults, which we often call volunteers. But, depending on their context, it could be anybody. If the influential adult that is investing in those kids - you invest in them.

If you're not finding a way to steadily invest in all three of those channels, then your stool won't stand. It won't hold anything up. You have to decide what you're going to do in those channels and how you're going to maintain a balance. You don't have to have equal investment in every leg at the same time.

Right.

But you do need to make sure that none of them are going without your attention, and you need to have a plan for how you're going to invest in each.

Okay. Let's go one layer deeper. What would be the elements of the plan that you would encourage a children's pastor to look at when it comes reaching kids?

The first thing I would say is, if you've already defined what you want them to learn and, you've defined the channels of how you're going to learn it, now you've got to decide "How do I teach kids the Bible?" So, that may come out in how you design your worship services, or your Sunday School classes, or your small groups, or things like that. Because you're saying, "Okay, Bible plus this channel."

The second example might be the parent. You're saying, "Okay, I want to equip kids with the Bible. I've got to go through the parent. That's my channel." So, what do you do? You encourage and equip the parent. You disciple them by telling them the value of investing this time in their children. You give them equipment of scripture, or tools, or resources. Whatever you think is appropriate for a parent to invest in their child, and then you find a way to circle back with that parent to see how that's going.

Third, with the influential adult, oftentimes those are your Sunday School teachers or your volunteers. So you want to make sure they feel comfortable and competent to do what they do, but they understand how what they're doing is fulfilling the Gospel, in both their life and the life of their child, in the children they invest in. Because when you do that, that's where you're going to get a lot more consistency and joy from the volunteer as they invest in the kids.

So in each case, you're saying, "Okay, I've got this scripture, this Gospel. I'm trying to get this to these kids. I'll do it this way directly to the children. This way in the hands of the parents. This way in the hands of the volunteers.

Okay. Good. Now, I know that one thing you and I talked about before this is the time that gets allotted in the week. Some people reading this are volunteers themselves.

Right.

They're at a church that's a really small church, and they are only half-time. And so, when you think about both developing a plan and implementing a plan – while everybody's context, again, is going to be different – what are some guidelines that can at least help them frame the conversation in their mind as far as how much time should be spent on the strategy? The developing of the plan? How much time, and I hate to even say percentages, because then some people are going to take that really legalistically. But what are those buckets that you think are important to evaluate as far as allotting time to developing strategy, the creativity piece, the planning the weekend, the volunteers, the parent, all those things?

I think you start with taking a realistic look at how kids are engaging in ministry today. To do that, I often look back at my childhood. I spent 24 hours a month in church. Four hours on Sunday, a couple hours on Wednesday, and then even random times in between for different things. That's time spent in God's Word, connecting with influential adults, and building relationships. Right? I watch, as a children's pastor, that 24 hours a month become 24 hours a year. Because families' attendance went from three or four times a week for a couple hours to twice a month for one hour. And that's it. So, you've got to realize that we cannot live in a world where what we were doing is always going to be what we are doing. Because things change.

Our reality is, on average, a children's pastor gets about half an hour a week with a kid, when you look at statistics. If that's the case, you can't put 90% of your effort into that one time. Because you're putting too much effort into a small amount of return. Whereas a parent is caring for their child at least seven hours a week. That's just specifically the parent taking care of the child! So, time you spend equipping parents to help disciple their kids increases that opportunity for the kid to come in and learn more about Christ. So you're accomplishing your goal.

I think the question you ask yourself is, "Okay, where are my children spending time?" The one analogy I use if you found out your ministry kids were spending half an hour at Chuck E. Cheese's® every week, where would you be eating your dinner? You'd be eating a lot of pizza! Getting to know those kids. So you find out, Where are my kids spending their time? How do I invest in the people in their lives in that time?

I think in order to do that, you have to put some boundaries. You have say to yourself, "I can't spend all of my time prepping for a weekend, because I have to spend some of my time investing in kids in this direction, and then some of my time investing in my kids through my volunteers." I don't want to put percentages on it, because to do that, I would have to assume I know your world, which I don't!

I would say you need to understand for yourself two key words: meaningful and memorable. If you've got a meaningful and memorable experience for your weekend planned – and it takes you a day – two days will not make it more meaningful and memorable! You won't get the return on your time that way. So, however much time you believe it takes to make your weekend experience meaningful and memorable for a child, that's a good boundary to put on it. And then put your creativity into another channel to create meaningful and memorable experiences through parents and through volunteers.

That's good. Meaningful and memorable. I think that's a good place to end. I haven't heard it put quite like that, but I like that idea of, "How do we make sure that it's meaningful and memorable, and not try to overdo it?

Right.

Well, thank you so much, Jason. I appreciate what you do for the kingdom, what you do for kids, and your creativity, and heart. I appreciate you taking the time to be with me today.

Thank you, Keith, I enjoyed it. I appreciate it.

Jason Tilley

Jason Tilley is the Co-Founder of Ministry Accelerator. Ministry Accelerator equips ministry leaders to navigate cultural complexity and experience fruitful ministry. Jason has led large, multi-site ministries, produced three children's ministry curricula, and oversaw the design of one of the first online discipleship tools. Currently, Jason is exploring ministry in the digital space and better team communication.

How do I effectively minister to millennial parents?

I am here today with Michayla, the Executive Director of the International Network of Children's Ministry. Thanks so much for joining me Michayla.

Thanks for having me Keith.

Before we dive into discussing millennial parents and serving them well, give us a little bit of your ministry journey when it comes to the children's and family ministry.

Sure. I joke that I don't really know any different. I grew up the child of a volunteer children's ministry director and my dad was the youth pastor in our small church. Children's ministry was just a regular part of our family. So I was volunteering at a very young age, serving in our children's church and bus ministry. I was a camp counselor probably a lot earlier than I should have been. [Laughs] I just grew up around it. I remember thinking, "Man, I wish there was someone who could come alongside and help my mom and dad."

I didn't even really know what I was asking for, but eventually God opened up a door for me to serve at a parachurch organization here in Chicago that serves children's ministry leaders and churches globally. That was 11 years ago. About four years ago, God brought me to the International Network of Children's Ministry where we get to do that! We get to come alongside leaders like my mom and dad and provide them with resources and training and equipping that they need. The Lord has just always had me in this community, and I love it dearly.

And we are blessed because you are in it for sure.

Thank you.

As we dive into millennial parents, define for us, for the context of this interview, what is a millennial and therefore their parents?

Sure. I think it's important to just remember when we talk about millennials as a generation, that generational cohorts are really designed as a tool to analyze changes and views over time. I think we can get a little bit distracted in that language, but just remember generational cohorts, like millennials, are just a tool to be able to understand a group of people. Pew Research landed in March that millennials are those who have been born between about 1981 to 1996. Typically, when I talk about millennials, I identify them as early 1980s babies to mid-1990s. Their parents were Boomers. They represent right now over a quarter of our nation's population.

Wow.

They're the most educated and most diverse generation. We also call them "digital natives" in that they grew up with technology, not immigrating to it as we talk about other generations. That's it, that's a broad overview of a millennial.

Yeah. I think even just hearing it in that quick a succession kind of had me thinking about some different things together that I hadn't thought about before: how educated...and diverse...and digital they are. I have heard about all of those things individually, but as you think about them together you start to get this picture. Speaking of thinking of things together, I know that INCM recently conducted a survey. What are some highlights of what you learned from that?

Absolutely. We were really curious, on behalf of the church, of what is happening right now in the minds and hearts of millennials who are now becoming parents. About 16.2 million millennials are moms now. So when you think about that as a group of parents, we're curious: What's on their minds? What's in their hearts? How does the church reach this group of families?

So, when we were digging into the survey, one of the things that was of specific interest to us was millennial parents of faith. Those who claim to have a Christian faith and desire to in some way be a part of the church and include their children in that. There were a lot of highlights from that, but I think one of the things that is really encouraging is that, of those surveyed, about 74% grew up in a Christian home, and 95% of that group said that their faith is important to them and it influences how they parent.

I just think that for us as leaders, and even as parents – if boomers are reading this, I hope they hear this as encouragement – the efforts we put into the spiritual formation of kids, even when we feel like it's not making a difference, it matters. And it has a lasting impact. And it's influencing how these parents are raising their kids and how they parent.

I think that's a huge encouragement we took away from the survey. Interestingly enough though, for these parents, 95% said that they want to see their children come to know, and love, and serve Jesus Christ. That's a big focus for them. But when we started to dig into their spiritual disciplines or spiritual rhythms as a family, that's where you begin to see the numbers get a little bit rocky. Only about 50% make Bible reading a regular priority.

If you just think about that in terms of my desire as a parent to disciple my child, but I am only in the Word a nominal amount of time, you can see what's going to happen there. Part of that is the millennial's faith journey and experience was very programmatic rather than relational discipleship teaching and modeling how these rhythms flow in and out of my everyday life. The church has a real opportunity there to come alongside millennial parents and help them understand spiritual disciplines is a way TO life, not a legalistic rhythm that's going to interrupt their regularly scheduled programming.

Right. I've said this is the first generation of parents that are being asked to, and want to, disciple their kids, but they were not discipled.

Absolutely.

So frequently, they're not equipped even when they want to be. As you've mentioned, and why we're talking about this, is where the church comes in. When it comes to connecting those millennial parents and their concerns and their desires with children's ministry at a church, what are those parents thinking about? What are they concerned about as it relates to children's ministry at the church?

Absolutely. I think the first place you have to start is thinking about who – I don't like to put it in these terms but just for clarity – think about who your audience is. Right? Unfortunately, and fortunately, with technology today, we have much more access, much more information, but also a greater influence of sweeping generalizations that can give us a less objective approach to beginning a relationship with someone in that generation.

The labels we've heard and projected onto them can really influence the way we approach and see this audience. But the truth is, I am not all of the memes about my generation on Facebook. Nor are the parents who are walking through the doors of the church! Understanding your audience doesn't necessarily mean that you know all of the sweeping generalizations about millennials. It's: do you know the millennials in your church? Have you actually had a conversation to understand their story, their background, where they're coming from? What's important to them? I think that's the first place to start. Get to know your audience. There are some practical ways we can do that, but I would for sure start there.

I think the other piece is we also know there are specific things that concern millennials regarding their children's church experience. One of the things that came out loud and clear from the survey was how critical safety and security was to millennial parents when they were bringing their child to the church and putting them in a children's ministry.

It's huge. It's something that we didn't even think about as kids. And not only did we not think about...our parents didn't think about either.

Absolutely.

But it's huge now.

I think about my children's ministry experience. It wasn't my personal experience as a child that I had a sticker on the back of my shirt because of a check in system. We just showed up and it felt very safe and secure. But if you think again about the backstory of the millennial experience, all of the things coming out about the media, deceit and abuse, and all of that, those things form the way that we see the world, how we see the church, and our experience of the church. So it's important as leaders in children's ministry and family ministry that we recognize it's on us to create a safe and secure environment for the kids in our ministry because they're the most vulnerable, and they also are the ones who don't have a voice to be able to speak up for themselves. We're their advocates. We're the ones who are there to make sure that they have a voice in that space.

Their parents, when they see that we care about that and that's an important priority for our church and our ministry, that is going to speak love to those parents. To know that you care that my child is safe, that there is a secure building, that things are child proof, that there are no dangerous chemicals they're going to get into, these volunteers have gone through multiple screenings... All of that helps me as a parent when I am handing you my child. To feel secure and safe as a mom to be able to put my child in your care. That is the number one thing. It doesn't matter if you're a small church or a large church. There needs to be safety and security measures across the board. It doesn't matter if there are ten kids or 1,000 kids. There needs to be safety and security in that church.

Huge. For sure.

Yeah.

No doubt about it. No doubt.

One other thing that stood out to us from the survey that was really important, the parents described it as the "ethos" of the children's ministry. I think as you dig into that word, a piece of it is environment, like the physical environment, how it looks and how it appears, but it's mostly about how it feels. When you think about the things that contributes to how I feel when I walk into a church building, it's everything from the volunteers to the lighting, to the décor, but also to my experience encountering that environment. One of the things that they highlight is that so many churches seemed to be geared toward 'insiders.'

For example, when I enter the church parking lot, do I know which door is closest to the children's ministry wing if I haven't been there before? When I walk into any door in the church building, do I know where to begin walking toward the children's ministry? When I get to the children's ministry area, where do I go as a first-timer to get my child checked in? If those things aren't obvious and clear, it can affect my experience of the ethos of that church. It can feel like I am an outsider, not one that is being welcomed into this community. That was another really, really big deal.

Oh, no doubt. I haven't heard it described as that, that "ethos" and the "feel" of the church. I've certainly had conversations about signage, and direction, and welcoming people, but to think about the overall feel of the church forces you to have a bigger conversation than just "do I have a clear sign? Oh yes. We do, so we must be good."

Absolutely.

What else? As we keep unpacking this, what are some other ways churches can better serve millennial parents?

There are a few things we've been really recommending to churches. Number one is to care about their marriage. What's interesting is if you look at the ways that millennials talk about marriage it's – the term that comes up most often – is "team." Mostly because with a lot of millennials, both spouses are working, and so they see their child-raising and home-owning, and all of those components as a team effort. I think that's really awesome that millennials are talking about marriage in terms of teamwork. As a church coming alongside that though, of saying, "Hey. We see you're moving at lightning speed. We want to give you guys an opportunity to go to Starbucks for an hour and sit across from each other and look each other in the eye. Bring the kids to church on Thursday night from 6:00 to 7:00 and go have a coffee date. And this one's on us."

Caring for their marriage is going to speak volumes to that millennial couple! That you recognize their child's spiritual formation is directly affected by the health of the home, and so providing an opportunity for that to happen. Millennials are a transient generation, so not everyone has family nearby to step in for babysitting and it can be expensive, so providing for that date night is a really practical simple way I think to show a millennial that you care about their marriage.

I think another piece within that is connecting them to other couples. As you get to know the millennial families in your children's ministry, and you start to understand what they care about and what their rhythms are, where you start to see connections, build those connections for the families in your church. Say, "You know what? I've been talking to Joe and Susan over here, and I just think that you guys are in this similar walk of life. I'd love to connect you. Can I do that?" Maybe have them both over for dinner, and spark that yourself. But being able to care for their families and connecting them to other couples is going to be really important. Sometimes saying, "Go get in a small group" is a little intimidating for millennials and their schedules. Sometimes you have to help them get into the 3-foot end of the pool before they jump all the way in.

Right.

Then I think noticing and encouraging. If they're holding hands, walking through the children's ministry wing, say, "Man, I just, I love the way that you guys love each other!" That took you two seconds, but it showed them you noticed them, and you were encouraging their affection for each other. That's a big deal. Really simple, not earth shattering, but those couple of things could really take things a new direction with those families.

Inviting. Inviting them in to the community of your church. Sometimes I think we want to go towards this big family event and put on this big production. Those have a place and they're valuable, but with millennials, authentic relationships are everything. Being able to say, "Hey, let's meet up for coffee," or "Come on over to my house for dinner." It would be really great, when they come over for dinner, if your house didn't look perfect! If there was maybe a Cheerio on the floor, or something that looks similar to their experience, that didn't feel intimidating, that would help. [Laughs]

One of my friends, Kim, she's a children's ministry leader in South Carolina. She will meet up with them in the places these millennial moms regularly go. Like a playground, or an indoor play place. So something like, "Hey, can I meet up with you and your kids on Thursday morning and just hang out?" That has been a game changer. She now has this moms' group, and they're encouraging each other, and other moms are meeting up on that Thursday morning. She has invited them into the church community while meeting them in the regular rhythms of their life. I think that's just awesome! That's a huge deal!

I think the last piece that I would really hang on is unconditionally loving their kids. That looks like the safety and security piece, like really giving attention and budget and focus on your safety and security policies and systems. But also, caring about how the volunteers treat the children and greet the parents. With most millennial parents having younger kids right now, if you have a 2-year-old experiencing separation anxiety, and it's the fifth Sunday they've shown up to the nursery screaming their heads off, and the volunteer looks like "Oh man Jacob's here again." What that does to the parents is it lets them know "I'm not welcome. We are not welcome anymore." When a parent picks up their child from the nursery, one of my friends Amber said this, when they're saying "How did they do today?", what they're really asking is, "Can we come back next week?"

Training your volunteers on "the welcome" and how they interact with parents, and how they interact with that child in the drop-off and the pick-up is critical. They're paying attention to how they're being treated and how their child is being treated. Even if the child was horrible, being able to say, "Hey, you know what I noticed about Jacob this week? He did such a good job sharing the train set with this other little boy over here. Good job mom." For that mom...knowing that her child was probably a disaster going in, she will carry that home that day as her gold star to put up on the refrigerator! Something went right! [Laughs]

Getting parents gold stars. That may be the perfect place to wrap up. I'm sitting here thinking "Okay. We could do 20 of these 15-minute interviews and fill an entire book about serving millennial parents!"

Good idea.

Maybe you and I will need to tackle that project! But this has been gold! From what you learned in the survey, to the focus on authentic relationships, to meeting them where they're at, and taking care of their marriage, and ethos. There's just so much to chew on! So, I really, really appreciate you taking the time, Michayla.

Absolutely. And any time that, if a leader listening or reading is interested in getting more information, or more tools, or more resources, I'm happy to be a help in that way. This is a big topic, and we could go on and on like you said, but hopefully these couple of tips will get you thinking in a new direction.

Absolutely. Thanks.

Awesome. Thanks Keith.

Michayla White

As the Executive Director for the International Network of Children's Ministry, Michayla oversees the ministry and provides guidance for initiatives that inspire and equip the kidmin community. For over a decade, she has had the privilege of serving in various aspects of the children's and family ministry community. Michayla married her best friend and childhood sweetheart. They are having a blast raising two little boys.

How do I develop a personal and ministry mission statement?

I'm here today with Courtney Wilson. Thank you so much for joining me.

Absolutely.

Before we jump in to what a mission statement is and how to use it, give us a little bit of your background. What's been your children's ministry journey up to this point? And what context do you serve in now?

Well, I did not grow up in a Christian home. So I didn't go to church as a child until I started asking to go to church when I was in 3rd Grade. My parents just took me to the closest church around the corner and I found my "home" in their children's ministry. And as I got older, I was always volunteering in their children's ministry. I actually went to the associate pastor at that church and asked her, in high school, "Is this something you can do as a job? Can you be a children's minister?" And she told me no, that I should be a doctor instead. And so I followed her advice and I actually went premed. In the midst of my senior year of high school, I started volunteering at a church that preached the Gospel, and I started volunteering with two-year-olds. They allowed me to help there as long as I was not in a teaching role. I ended up having people invest in my life that led me to Christ. So when I went off to school to be a doctor, I was one year in, and felt like God was calling me to do something different, to go back to that original dream of children's ministry. I transferred up to the University of Northwestern in St Paul, Minnesota, and started working at a large church there.

We were a mobile church so we were in and out every weekend. I held a couple different positions there, one in early childhood and one where I instructed and wrote a program for 5th and 6th graders in that church. When I graduated from college, we moved to Arizona and I worked at a pretty well-established church of about a thousand people down there in Phoenix. I loved it, but my husband needed to finish school, so we went back to the church I had served at in Minnesota. And I was their elementary pastor for about a year and a half while my husband finished school.

At that point, we moved to Ohio. We were at a small church in Ohio. A very small church! I did the children's ministry there while I was a stay at home mom at the same time. So, bi-vocational years of being home with my little kids and also working in a smaller church. My husband as the youth pastor there, and it became obvious we were no longer a fit for that church, so we "sat out" of ministry for a few months to re-assess where God was calling us. I ended up going back to that church in Arizona again! I kind of had a back-and-forth journey.

I did a one-year interim there as their children's pastor to kind of help them clean up some things. They had had some hard years as the church. I was able to go in and just be generous with the leadership for a year there. I ended up in the Pacific Northwest after that, at another church of about a thousand in Vancouver, Washington. After that, ended up kind of feeling the need to be back in the Midwest with my family and ended up here, where I am now at Christ Community Church, which is a large, multi-site. I'm the elementary pastor here and I'm considered the lead director for elementary. I set vision and pace for 1st through 5th Grade at all of our campuses, but I specifically oversee it at our largest campus, which is here in St. Charles, IL.

Before we dive into how to use a mission statement, why should somebody even have a mission statement?

Well…I believe a mission statement allows you to say, "Yes" to things and to say, "No" to things. It gives you kind of your guard rails and your map for where you're going. If you have a mission statement, then you know what you can say, "Yes" to and what you can say, "No" to because it lines up with where you're going and what you said you're going to be about.

Good point! Because in children's ministry, people aren't necessarily struggling with what to say, "Yes" to. They're struggling with what to say, "No" to. And having that clear vision certainly helps.

Yes.

I know that with mission statements, most people just kind of think, "Oh yea…we have a mission statement." But you actually believe in three types of mission statements, so unpack that for a second.

I think that, especially in children's ministry because we sit in this kind of "second chair" area, we really work with three different kinds of mission statements. We should all have a personal mission statement. I tell people, "Your personal mission statement is what you do no matter where you are." So, when I'm a children's pastor, when I'm a mom, when I'm a wife, when I'm a friend, whatever role I play, there's a mission statement that guides me. There's something that allows me to say yeses and there's something that allows me to say nos.

Personally, my personal mission statement is that I'm all about "encouraging and equipping." So, when I am planning a family vacation, I'm encouraging and equipping. When I'm coaching my kids in how to do their homework, I'm encouraging and equipping. When I'm listening to my husband download his day, I'm encouraging and I'm equipping. But also, when I'm standing in front of a group of volunteers, I'm encouraging and I'm equipping. When I'm working with my staff team – I oversee a couple of full time staff and a part time staff – then I am encouraging and equipping them.

That personal mission statement guides me, helps me to know what my identity is, who I am and what I'm good at, no matter where I go.

Then we also…we work under the authority of a church. So, we have a church mission statement. Frequently, our churches have thought of these beautiful statements. They're generally either quite concise or sometimes quite verbose. [Laughs] We have something that guides what our church is about, that allows our church say, "Yes" and to say, "No" to certain things.

And then, falling under that, we have our children's ministry mission statement. It might match up exactly word-for-word with your church's mission statement, which actually I think is a pretty important thing, or it may be something separate that still is that guiding force. What is it that tells you what you can say "Yes" to and what you should say "No" to?

Once you have those mission statements: You've got your personal one. You've got the church one. You've got the children's ministry one...either lining up exactly or certainly being very complimentary, hand-in-glove. How does that practically, on a daily basis, on a yearly basis, how does that get used by you in your role in leading the children's ministry?

I think that, again, there's first that personal piece. I know that – because I'm all about encouraging and equipping – I might need to find some people who have a different mission statement than I do. People who say, "I am here because I like to put plans to people's vision." I like to find those people because I'm pretty good at encouraging and equipping, but when you ask me to put the day to day timeline to things, you ask me to project plan, that's not going to be my strong point! I'm going to need to find some people that I can surround myself with who have mission statements that are complementary to mine.

In your ministry life, whether that be staff that you're hiring or volunteers – high capacity volunteers that you're equipping around you or that you call up to come and work with you – to really call mission out in people and ask them, "What are you about no matter where you are?" It's a big deal to people!

It helps them to see their value and to see how you can complement each other. How you need them to complete your ministry, to do ministry in the context of the church.

That second type of mission statement is your church mission statement. When we look at the church mission statement overall and we look at how it filters down into our children's ministry statement, well, all of these big things that the church is doing and what your church is about, it's going to filter down into who you are.

I mean, if your church is about having certain "care" ministries and they need childcare, well that just became part of your mission too as a children's ministry. So, knowing what your church's mission statement is, and helping your leadership to stay accountable to that as well. Because we are all about "shiny things" in ministry. Sometimes without a mission statement, we lose sight of that a little bit. And so, in the larger church, it's necessary to have some buy-in to, "Hey, this is really what we are about as a church." That needs to guide who we are as a church. Those things are going to trickle down then into your children's ministry.

Which brings us to the third type of mission statement we deal with, and that's your children's ministry mission statement. Again, I tend to think your children's ministry mission statement should match your church's mission statement, so that you are taking these tiny humans that you are leading, and doing the same things with them that you are with the adults in your ministry. I also think that gives you a lot of buy-in with your senior leadership! If you can say, "This is what we are about," you don't have to work to have them understand your mission statement. They get it because it's their mission statement. So it makes sense when they fit really, really well together. If they're not exact, again, like you said, hand-in-glove, something that really, really fits together so that your senior leadership understands what you're about. But then as a children's ministry, how does that guide everything you do?

That's your yeses and nos. That's your goals for the year. When you look and you set out to make goals and to figure out what your ministry is going to be about in a year, if you have a mission statement that guides that, it should be pretty easy to set your goals off of that. When you select curriculum for your ministry, it should be easy to select your curriculum based upon what you've said your mission statement is, what you've said you're going to be about. So, when we are about the things that we've said we are going to be about, then it's going to make it easier to lead each aspect of our ministry moving forward.

In the last couple of minutes, as I've heard you talk about the different areas, whether it be dealing with senior leadership or choosing curriculum for training people, you've mentioned many times this idea of a mission statement makes it easier. I think that's something to kind of hammer home a little bit. So often, people don't create, or focus on, or vision-cast based on a mission statement, because it feels like it's going to be too much work. And if they actually do it for a year or two, they'll realize how much time is saved. Significantly more time gets saved in living out the mission statement than it takes to plan it. As I was thinking about having that clear mission statement sitting right in front of you as you're communicating with senior leadership, as you mentioned, that conversation becomes easier. And so, the amount of stress and prep you have to put into communicating something to senior leadership, you won't have to spend that level of time and effort because you already have common language, so to speak. The little bit of extra work upfront makes a whole lot of other things easier. For sure.

Now, this may take us off in a little bit of a tangent, but you mentioned goal setting. In this context of having a mission statement, I'd love to hear a little bit about your goal setting process. Not just as it ties to mission statements, but what's the rhythm of that? When do you do it? What do you include in that process? I know that goal setting is really important to you and your ministry team. It would be really helpful, having just had the conversation we had, to hear a little bit about how kind of rubber meets the road from a goal setting standpoint.

Personally, I set goals. I try to go every six months where I'll sit down and I'll look at my personal mission statement. I'm here to encourage and equip. And I look at: What's going right with that? What's going wrong? What's confused? And what's missing? Those are the four questions I ask myself. And so personally I'll write my own goals based upon that.

What am I doing really well? What am I not doing well? Where do I need to play on strengths and where do I need to shore up the weaknesses?

But then as a ministry, we set goals annually. We do our goals with our fiscal year. We'll take that children's ministry mission statement, which again always lines up with the church's: To make passionate disciples of Jesus Christ who are belonging, growing, serving and reaching. We sit down as a staff team and we brainstorm, again, what's going right? What's wrong or not working well? What's confused or we feel like there's confusion around it? And what's missing? What might be a little bit of dreaming or things that we might want to see?

A couple years ago, we actually took our mission statement, which handily breaks down into four marks of a disciple: belonging, growing, serving, and reaching. As a staff team, we just took time to dream. We wrote big lists of all of the things we would want to see in the area of helping kids belong, helping kids grow, helping kids serve, helping kids reach. What's that going to look like?

In each one of those four areas, we came up with this big document of ways that we could do that. Again, in a multisite setting, it has to be "If it's good for one campus, it should be good for the other campuses."

That document, to this day, drives our goals every year. We go back through that document every year. I think this is our third year we've gone back through it and said, "What have we still not done that we dreamt about three years ago that lined up with our mission statement that could be a part of our goals in this next year?"

As a church, we set church goals, all-church goals. Those feed into what we call our "team goals." Those team goals are the ones that we use as a children's ministry team, and then those will feed down into individual goals.

Some of those mission statement goals that we wrote out a couple of years ago, have come up into our personal goals each year. There have been some of those that have shown up, like creating a resource that helps communicate the Gospel to kids that small group leaders can use. Well…that's a "reaching" thing for us. We want our kids to know how to evangelize. We want our leaders to be good at communicating the Gospel. That was an easy goal to set for me because I knew that it fed into our mission statement.

So, it's really this "trickle down" of, "How do we take the bigger mission statement and ask the right questions and move it into the right goals?" And then how are those "SMART" goals? Everybody's probably has heard of SMART goals. Goals that are specific and measurable and all of those things. Do these goals all make sense in the context of our ministry?

Again, we get to say, "No" to some things that don't fit our mission statement, and then we get to say enthusiastic yeses and know that we will have support from leadership on some of those big dreams, because we know they feed into our greater mission statement as well.

That's great. This has been fantastic to focus on, and unpack a bit, the need for a mission statement, how that feeds into doing goals and even our thought process and simplifying how we do ministry by giving us those guard rails. I like that image of the guard rails of yes and no. So thanks so much for taking the time to unpack this with us a bit.

No problem.

Courtney Wilson

Courtney Wilson is the Elementary Pastor at Christ Community Church in St Charles, IL. She has been serving in children's ministry for 19 years.. She loves encouraging and equipping parents to find joy in raising kids who know and love God and have faith in Jesus. Courtney's favorite role is being mom to three amazing sons and an awesome daughter, and can often be heard as the loudest mom during their cross country races.

KEITH FERRIN

Keith Ferrin is an author, speaker, storyteller, and blogger. Actually, that's more of what he "does." As far as who he is...He is a disciple of Jesus Christ, a husband to Kari (world's most outstanding wife), and a father to Sarah, Caleb, and Hannah (the three coolest – and craziest – kids on the planet). Keith is also a coffee drinker, ice cream eater, youth soccer coach (who occasionally makes the mistake of thinking his body can still do what it did when he was 17), amateur guitar player, lover of twisty-turny movies, and eater of almost any kind of food (except olives). You can find Keith in Seattle where he is the happy guy hanging out with his wife and kids doing something fun in the outdoors. You can also catch him online at KeithFerrin.com.

Let's Connect

I love to connect with my readers. Truly. Shoot me an email. I'll write back. There are lots of ways we can connect. Here are a few:

Email: Keith@KeithFerrin.com

Blog: KeithFerrin.com

On your favorite social media @KeithFerrin

And if you have a question, comment, or idea for another book, or a topic you'd like me to write about on the blog, please shoot me a note.

I'd love to hear from you.

Enjoy More Books and Resources by Keith Ferrin

Like Ice Cream

What if passing on a love for God's Word could be as natural – and enjoyable – as passing on a love for ice cream? I believe it can be. When it comes to creating an environment in which the next generation is most likely to fall in love with the Bible, the principles are surprisingly similar to the way a love for ice cream gets passed on from generation to generation. Whether you are a parent, youth pastor, children's pastor – or anyone who cares deeply about the next generation – you will find Like Ice Cream to be filled with encouragement and practical ideas you can start using today.

Bible Praying for Parents

As parents, we *want* to pray for our kids. We know we *should* pray for them. And yet, our prayers often feel repetitive. Or we wonder if they're making a difference. We know there is power in praying God's Word. We know His Word is in line with God's will. And we know it covers every aspect of life. Bible Praying for Parents will help with three sections that focus on praying Scripture for your child: 365 Daily Prayers, Bible Prayers by Category, and 40 Blessings to Pray straight from God's Word. It's the ultimate resource for Bible Praying for your child.

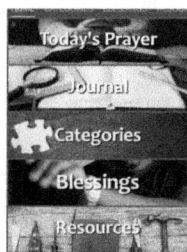

Bible Praying App for smart phones

Bible Praying for Parents is also an app available wherever you buy your favorite phone apps! Have easy, daily access to Bible prayers you can personalize for your child and even share on social media. Get daily notifications to remind you to pray. Bible Praying will help you get started – and stay consistent – in daily, powerful prayer for your child.

How to Enjoy Reading Your Bible

Do you feel like you should read the Bible more?

This book will help you want to read it.

Keith Ferrin has been talking to churches for years about enjoying God's Word. Here he shares the most helpful ideas and habits you can start using today. You will find ten proven tips that are equally practical whether you are a longtime Bible student or simply exploring what this life-changing book is all about.

These books and more are available on Amazon.com or wherever you buy books and ebooks.

Find more books, courses, and free resources at KeithFerrin.com

www.ingramcontent.com/pod-product-compliance
Lightning Source LLC
LaVergne TN
LVHW051402080426
835508LV00022B/2944